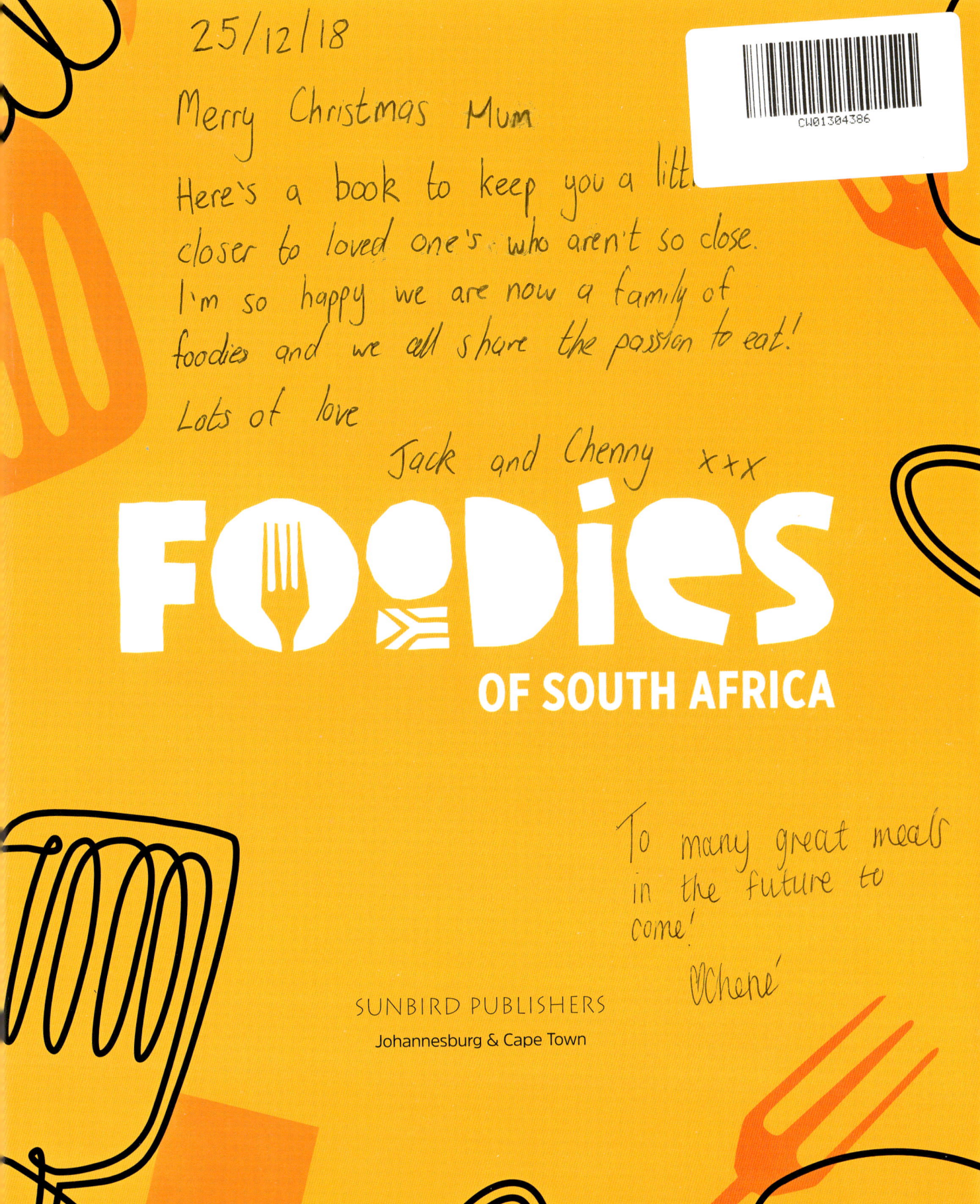

25/12/18

Merry Christmas Mum

Here's a book to keep you a little closer to loved one's who aren't so close. I'm so happy we are now a family of foodies and we all share the passion to eat!

Lots of love

Jack and Chenny xxx

FOODIES
OF SOUTH AFRICA

To many great meals in the future to come!

Chené

SUNBIRD PUBLISHERS
Johannesburg & Cape Town

FOODIES
OF SOUTH AFRICA

THE MOST VIRAL
RECIPES EVER!

COMPILED BY CHANTAL BOTHA, HAYLEY MURISON, JULIE BROWN

Sunbird Publishers
Johannesburg & Cape Town

This book is dedicated to Lauren Ratcliffe. The most awesome wife any guy could have.
– Jon Ratcliffe (Jon is the founder of Engage Video Group, the company behind Foodies of South Africa. He has worked closely with the rest of the team to bring this book to life.)

CONTENTS

8 From on-screen inspiration to go-to guide in the kitchen

10 TOP 10 MOST VIRAL RECIPES

32 BREAKFAST BITES

48 SAVOURY

Quick bites 50
Mains 74
On the braai ... 130

142 SWEET STUFF

188 DRINKS

INDEX 218

KEY

 Total views

 Total shares

 Likes

 Vegetarian meals

 Nonalcoholic drinks

From on-screen inspiration
TO GO-TO GUIDE IN THE KITCHEN

'Looks soooo delicious ... YUMMY ... Sure gonna make these sometime!'

These are just some of the comments our fans share daily in the Foodies of SA online world.

Thank you, Mzansi! Such heartfelt reactions to our videos are what we live for in the Foodies team. They stir us to continue inspiring with creative and often uniquely South African recipe ideas, like *Pap in a Pumpkin*, *Croque Meneer* and *Amarula Rooibos Latte* – to name a few!

Where did this food journey begin, you might wonder?

What started out two years ago as a two-foodie team with a big dream has grown into a vibrant and thriving community of South Africa's most passionate food lovers.

Our foodie friends have watched our easy-to-follow videos hundreds of millions of times ... and many of them have gone on to share them on their own Facebook timelines. In fact, our research shows that Foodies of SA videos have had more shares and video views *than any other social media page in Southern Africa*!

We've been blown away by the support and positive feedback from our community and get so excited when our fans post pictures or videos of their creations that we've inspired. Most of all, we love it when people connect with their loved ones over our recipes.

This idea of sincere connection between friends and family is the fuel that drives everything that we do. To us, food is much more than *just* food. Food is an intimate and intricate part of one's life story – it is belonging, heritage, culture ... and connection.

While our fantastic foodie fans love connecting with friends and family by sharing our yummy recipe clips online, many of those same food lovers have been asking us to put together a book of our most popular recipes: something tangible, durable, gift-able and beautiful that will become a trusty go-to guide in the kitchen for many years to come.

Well, here it is! This book is a very real embodiment of our mission, which is to sustain meaningful relationships and sincere connections by revitalising the act of everyday cooking and sharing.

We hope you'll find our book inspiring, and that it will become a much-consulted, often-shared, dog-eared, flour-dusted, time-worn kitchen companion that has a special spot in your home and in your heart.

The recipes in this cookbook are based on our short how-to video clips. However, some recipes have been slightly edited to ensure the best possible result for you.

So from us to you ... A big thank you and ENJOY!

**The Team at
Foodies of South Africa**

Mac 'n Cheese Burger
(recipe on page 92)

THE TOP 10 MOST VIRAL RECIPES

CHEESY EGG TOASTY

An easy way to make a delicious brekkie for the family,
your digs mates or the rugby team!

4 slices Sasko Premium white bread
4 eggs
Butter for spreading
1–2 cups grated cheddar cheese
Salt and pepper
2 tsp oil
8 rashers bacon
250 g button mushrooms
1 clove garlic, diced
2 tsp Sasko cake flour
1 cup cream
Avocado

Views: 37 156 204

Likes: 1 033 552

Shares: 668 173

1. Using a spoon, indent the centre of each bread slice to create a square shape.

2. Crack an egg into the centre of each bread slice.

3. Butter the edges of the bread slices and top with grated cheese and salt and pepper to taste.

4. Bake for 5–10 minutes at 180°C.

5. Add 2 teaspoons oil to a skillet, and fry the bacon rashers until crispy.

6. Remove the bacon and place wiped and chopped button mushrooms in the pan with salt and pepper to taste.

7. Brown the mushrooms before adding diced garlic, flour and cream. Allow the sauce to thicken while stirring continuously.

8. Serve the egg sarmie topped with avocado slices, creamy mushroom sauce and bacon rashers.

STEP 1 Crack an egg into each slice and top edges with grated cheese.

STEP 2 Fry the bacon rashers in a pan. Then make a sauce with mushrooms, garlic, flour and cream.

STEP 3 Bake the egg toasties.

TOP 10 MOST VIRAL RECIPES | 13

S'MORES DIP

Fluffy marshmallows melted on a silky smooth chocolate and caramel base. This might just be the best braai idea of ALL TIME.

2 slabs Beacon milk chocolate
1 tbsp butter
Wilson's cream caramels
Beacon marshmallows (white and pink)
Vanilla biscuits for dipping

Views: 1 042 506
Likes: 30 431
Shares: 25 041

1. Preheat a pan in the Weber.
2. Roughly chop the milk chocolate slabs.
3. Remove the pan from the Weber and melt the butter in the pan.
4. Add the chocolate pieces to the pan, allowing them to melt slightly.
5. Lay the cream caramels over the chocolate.
6. Layer the white and pink marshmallows over the chocolate and caramel, making sure to cover all the gaps.
7. Bake in the Weber at 180°C for 5–7 minutes.
8. Serve with vanilla biscuits for dipping.

STEP 1 Melt butter in a pan and add chopped chocolate slabs.

STEP 2 Lay the cream caramels over the chocolate.

STEP 3 Layer white and pink marshmallows over the mixture.

PANCAKE CAKE

If you can make one pancake, you can make this epic rainbow pancake cake!

FOR THE PANCAKES
3 eggs
4 cups milk
4 tbsp oil
1 tsp Moir's vanilla essence
3 cups Sasko cake flour
1 tsp Moir's baking powder
Moir's food colouring (4 different colours)
Oil for frying pancakes

FOR THE ICING
3 x 230 g tubs cream cheese or smooth cottage cheese
6 tbsp yoghurt
½ cup Huletts icing sugar

FOR SERVING
Fresh raspberries
2–3 tsp icing sugar

1. In a large bowl, combine the eggs, milk, oil and vanilla essence.
2. Sift the cake flour and baking powder into this mixture.
3. Blend together until smooth using a mixer.
4. Divide equal amounts of the pancake batter between four bowls and add a different colour of food colouring to each bowl. Mix until combined.
5. Add more food colouring as needed.
6. Heat oil in a pan and fry the pancakes.
7. For the icing, blend cream cheese with yoghurt and icing sugar until smooth.
8. Spread the icing over each of the pancakes and stack them one on top of the other.
9. Ice the top of the pancake cake and garnish with fresh raspberries and a dusting of icing sugar.
10. Slice and serve.

Views: 695 342

Likes: 19 232

Shares: 11 264

TOP 10 MOST VIRAL RECIPES | 17

HASH BROWN
BREAKFAST PIZZA

A delightfully cheesy breakfast pizza that's gluten-free, grain-free, easy to make and an absolute crowd pleaser!

FOR THE HASH BROWN BASE
2 large potatoes, peeled
2 large Food Lover's Market eggs
½ cup grated Food Lover's Market cheddar
Salt
Pepper

FOR THE PIZZA TOPPING
6 rashers Food Lover's Market streaky bacon, cut into pieces
½ cup grated Food Lover's Market cheddar
4 large Food Lover's Market eggs
1 cup mushrooms, chopped
Chopped fresh chives, for garnish

1. To make the hash browns, grate the potatoes into a large bowl filled with cold water. Stir until the water is cloudy, drain and cover the potatoes again with fresh cold water. Stir again to dissolve excess starch. Drain potatoes well, pat dry with paper towels and squeeze out any excess moisture.

2. Stir in 2 eggs, ½ cup grated cheddar and salt and pepper to taste.

3. Preheat oven to 180°C. Line a baking tray with baking paper and add the hash brown mixture. Using your hands, pat the mixture into a rectangular shape. Bake for about 20 minutes, until golden.

4. While the hash brown crust is baking, cook the bacon in a large pan over medium heat until crispy, about 6 minutes per side.

5. Top the baked crust with the remaining ½ cup cheddar and crack the remaining 4 eggs on top. Scatter with crumbled bacon and chopped mushrooms and season all over with salt and pepper.

6. Bake until the egg whites are set but the yolks are runny, 8–12 minutes.

7. Garnish with chives, slice and serve.

STEP 1 Grate the potatoes and stir in eggs and cheese.

STEP 2 Pat the mixture into a rectangular shape and bake.

STEP 3 Crack eggs onto hash brown crust and add remaining ingredients.

Views:
986 850

Likes:
22 385

Shares:
21 873

AMARULA
STICKY MALVA PUDDINGS

A comforting classic + AMARULA = a doubly delicious dessert idea!

1 cup sugar
1 egg
2 tbsp butter
1 tbsp apricot jam
1 cup flour
1 tsp bicarbonate of soda
½ cup milk
1 tsp vinegar
½ cup Amarula

FOR THE SAUCE:
1 cup caster sugar
½ cup melted butter
⅔ cup cream
Pinch of salt
½ cup Amarula

Vanilla ice cream, to serve

> Fantastic warm with melting ice cream. I believed it's passed by the Heart Foundation, so safe to eat.
> — **ROBERT KELLY**

1. In a large mixing bowl, beat the sugar and egg with a hand-held mixer.

2. Add the butter, apricot jam, flour and bicarbonate of soda to the mixture. Stir to combine.

3. Once combined, add milk, vinegar and ½ cup Amarula to the bowl and mix until smooth.

4. Place cupcake liners into the 12 cups of a muffin tin. Pour the mixture into the cupcake liners, filling each two-thirds of the way to the top.

5. Bake for 15–20 minutes at 180° C. Cool for 10 minutes and then remove.

6. While the puddings are baking, make the sauce. Heat caster sugar, melted butter and cream in a saucepan over a medium heat to make the sauce.

7. Bring the mixture to a boil. Once boiling, add a pinch of salt and the remaining ½ cup Amarula.

8. Keep the sauce on the heat until it caramelises.

9. Once caramelised, divide half of the sauce between the puddings, allowing it to soak in. Reserve the remaining sauce for serving with the puddings.

10. Serve each pudding with a scoop of vanilla ice cream and the reserved sauce.

 **Views:** 513 814

 **Likes:** 9 993

 **Shares:** 9 625

SPAGHETTI PIZZA

Quick, easy, affordable and DELICIOUS ... this creative dinner idea is bound to become a family favourite!

250 g Fatti's & Moni's spaghetti
2 eggs
¼ cup grated parmesan
1 cup marinara sauce
1 cup grated mozzarella cheese
Fresh basil leaves

1. Bring the spaghetti to the boil in lightly salted water.
2. Once cooked, drain and set aside.
3. Add the beaten eggs and grated parmesan to the spaghetti and stir to combine.
4. Spread the spaghetti out evenly on a greased baking tray.
5. Spread marinara sauce over the spaghetti and top with grated mozzarella cheese.
6. Bake at 220°C for 15 minutes or until the cheese is golden and crispy.
7. Serve with fresh basil leaves.

*Easy-peasy! I can do this!
Now just add a bottle of wine and good friends and bingo — success.*
— **BARB MEISNER**

 Views: 698 468   **Likes:** 13 892   **Shares:** 8 704

SHEET PAN PANCAKES

The easiest way to make pancakes for a crowd … and they're SO GOOD!

2 ⅕ cups milk
2 tbsp vegetable oil
2 extra-large eggs
1 x 500 g packet Sasko flapjack mix
1 cup strawberries
2 bananas
¾ cup blueberries
Icing sugar (optional)
Honey (optional)

1. Whisk the milk, vegetable oil and eggs in a large mixing bowl.

2. Gradually add the flapjack mix to the liquid mixture, whisking it thoroughly until lump free.

3. Pour the batter onto a baking paper-lined baking sheet and spread it to the edges.

4. Slice the strawberries and bananas.

5. Place the strawberry slices on top of the batter, followed by the banana slices and blueberries.

6. Bake at 180°C for 15 minutes, or until golden brown.

7. Sprinkle a dusting of icing sugar over the pancake before slicing.

8. Cut the pancake into squares and serve immediately with a drizzle of honey.

 **Views:** 458 525   **Likes:** 10 921   **Shares:** 10 295

CROQUE MENEER

A South African spin on a French classic – any cheese-lover's dream!

2 tbsp butter
2 tbsp Sasko cake flour
2 cups milk
2 cups grated cheese
Salt and pepper to taste
8 slices Sasko Low GI Dumpy Oats & Honey Flavoured white bread
Butter, for spreading
Dijon mustard, for spreading
Grated cheese
1–2 cups sliced biltong

Views: 1 725 793
Likes: 45 593
Shares: 33 651

1. Melt the butter in a pan. Once it is melted, add the flour and whisk until smooth.
2. Add the milk, stirring continuously until it thickens. Remove from the heat and add ½ cup of grated cheese, salt and pepper.
3. Toast the slices of bread. Line a baking tray with baking paper.
4. Place four toasted slices on the baking tray. Spread each with a thin layer of butter, followed by a generous layer of Dijon mustard.
5. Top with grated cheese and a few slices of biltong.
6. Add more cheese and place a slice of toast on top.
7. Pour the cheesy white sauce over the now closed sandwiches before topping with a final layer of grated cheese.
8. Bake at 180°C until golden brown.
9. Top with biltong slices and serve.

Made and devoured. Delish.
— GLENDA MARITZ

SANDWICH CAKE

A ginormous sarmie that looks like a cake ... SO COOL!

- 28 slices Sasko premium white bread
- 3 x 230 g tubs cream cheese or creamed cottage cheese
- 1 cucumber, sliced
- 500 g tomatoes or cherry tomatoes, thinly sliced
- 8 ham slices, rectangular
- 1 punnet chives
- Cherry tomatoes, halved
- Radish slices
- Fresh herbs

Views: 5 995 445

Likes: 197 420

Shares: 108 028

1. Cut the crusts off the bread slices.
2. Use the first four slices of bread to form a square bread base for the cake.
3. Spread cream cheese over the base and top with a layer of cucumber slices.
4. Make another layer of four slices of bread on top of the first and again spread cream cheese over the slices. Top with thinly sliced tomatoes.
5. Repeat with a layer of bread topped with cream cheese and ham slices.
6. Repeat the three layers. End with a layer of bread slices. There will be 7 layers in total.
7. Place a dinner plate on top of the layered bread slices and, using a very sharp knife, cut around the edges for a round cake shape.
8. Spread the remaining cream cheese over the whole bread cake, essentially 'icing' the cake with cream cheese.
9. Place the chives around the cake, sticking them to the cream cheese.
10. Garnish the top of the cake with cherry tomatoes, radish slices and fresh herbs.
11. Slice and serve.

STEP 1 Top bread base with cream cheese and cucumber slices.

STEP 2 Top second layer with cream cheese and thinly sliced tomatoes.

STEP 3 Top the third layer with cream cheese and ham.

STEP 4 'Ice' the entire sandwich cake with cream cheese.

You guys make us kitchen geniuses! Thank you!
— **THABISO NDEBELE**

STEP 1 Stir the butter into the melted chocolate.

STEP 2 Beat the eggs and sugar until thick and pale yellow.

STEP 3 Pour the batter into the 4 buttered and dusted ramekins.

MOLTEN AERO LAVA CAKES
WITH BAR-ONE SAUCE

Molten Aero puddings + a dreamy Bar-One sauce = a real-life CHOCOLATE EXPLOSION!

FOR THE LAVA CAKES
Butter for ramekins
Dark unsweetened cocoa powder for dusting
120 g Aero milk chocolate
120 g butter, diced
3 eggs
100 g granulated sugar
50 g cake flour

FOR THE BAR-ONE SAUCE
100 g Bar-One chocolate bars
½ cup cream

FOR SERVING
Vanilla ice cream (optional)
Areo milk chocolate

Views: 521 969

Likes: 9 826

Shares: 12 011

Lava cakes

1. Butter 4 individual ramekins and dust liberally with cocoa powder. Set aside.

2. Melt the Aero milk chocolate in a bowl over hot water.

3. Stir the butter into the chocolate until it melts. Set aside for 10 minutes to cool.

4. In another bowl, beat the eggs and sugar until thick and pale yellow.

5. Stir in the melted chocolate and butter mixture.

6. Fold in the flour and mix everything together. Divide the mixture among the 4 ramekins. Place the filled ramekins in the freezer for 10 minutes.

7. Preheat the oven to 200°C. Bake the chilled, filled ramekins for 12 minutes until the cake is cooked but the centre is still soft.

8. Remove from the oven and allow to rest for 3 minutes before you turn the ramekins upside down and empty the cakes onto dessert plates.

9. Serve warm with a scoop of vanilla ice cream. Drizzle with melted Bar-One sauce and chunks of Aero milk chocolate.

Bar-One sauce

1. Bring water to the boil in a big pot, and put a bowl or a pan on top of it.

2. Cut the chocolate bars into small pieces and place them in the bowl or pan.

3. Add the cream bit by bit and stir well until the sauce is melted and creamy.

> We made this recipe and it's absolutely sinful. Love every bit of it – so simple and easy to make!
> **– MASHA ARNOLD**

BREAKFAST BITES

BACON-WRAPPED BREAKFAST STACK

THE BEST BREAKFAST IDEA EVER!

FOR THE FLAPJACKS
2 tbsp vegetable oil
2 ⅕ cup milk
2 extra-large eggs
1 packet Sasko flapjack mix
Oil for frying

FOR SERVING
1 onion, sliced
250 g mushrooms
Cheddar cheese, sliced
2 packs (200 g each) streaky bacon
Eggs for frying

> Oooo, kwyl ek nou sommer. Dit is 'n awesome idee. Geen restaurant sal so iets bedien nie.
> – ADRIANA BONTHUYS JORDAAN

1. Preheat the oven to 180°C.

2. To make the flapjacks, beat the oil, milk and eggs together with a whisk in a bowl.

3. Gradually add the flapjack mix to the egg mixture and beat thoroughly with a whisk until lump free.

4. Use a tablespoon to spoon the mixture onto a hot, well-greased frying pan. Turn halfway through the frying process and fry until golden brown.

5. Caramelise the onions and mushrooms in a little oil until golden brown and sweet and set aside.

6. To assemble, layer 1 flapjack, 1 slice of cheese and a spoonful of caramelised onions and mushrooms. Top with another cheese slice and another flapjack.

7. Wrap 2 streaky bacon rashers around each flapjack until covered, securing the bacon with a toothpick if needed.

8. Bake the bacon-wrapped flapjacks in the oven for 15–20 minutes or until the bacon is crispy. Cover with foil if the flapjacks brown before the bacon is cooked.

9. Just before the bacon-wrapped flapjacks are ready, fry an egg sunny-side up (one per stack).

10. Remove the bacon-wrapped flapjack stack from the oven and place a fried egg on top of each stack.

11. Serve and slice open to reveal the hidden cheesy flapjack centre.

NOTE: You could keep the remaining flapjack batter in the fridge and fry them the next day, or use all the flapjack mixture and keep the fried flapjacks for the next day. Alternatively, you could freeze the batter, or even the fried flapjacks!

BOVRIL FRENCH TOAST
ROLL-UPS

The humble Bovril and cheese sarmie reimagined in a fun new way!

6 slices Sasko white bread
Bovril
Ham slices
Mozzarella cheese
6 eggs
Butter for frying

1. Cut the crusts off each slice of bread.

2. Flatten the bread slices with a rolling pin.

3. Spread Bovril evenly over each bread slice.

4. Place a ham slice on each bread slice.

5. Cut a thin finger of mozzarella cheese, no wider than the width of the slice of bread.

6. Place the mozzarella on one side of each slice of bread to roll (do not place it on the edge of bread, leave some room for rolling).

7. Roll up each bread slice tightly around the cheese, making sure it is tight and secure for frying.

8. Mix the eggs together in a bowl. Dip each Bovril roll-up in the egg mixture, making sure it is completely covered.

9. Heat some butter in a pan. Fry each Bovril roll-up until the cheese is melted and the bread is golden brown.

10. Remove from the pan and place on a rack or paper towels. Allow to cool and serve.

BREAKFAST BAGUETTE

Comparable to a massive breakfast fry-up ... but sooo much simpler!

1 Food Lover's Market baguette
Food Lover's Market cheddar cheese, grated
5 eggs
Salt and pepper to taste
1 punnet mushrooms
200 g Food Lover's Market streaky bacon
Cherry tomatoes
1 can of Food Lover's Market baked beans
Food Lover's Market olive oil
Avocado, sliced

1. Using a knife, cut 5 holes in the centre of the baguette.

2. Sprinkle grated cheddar cheese into each hole.

3. Crack an egg into each hole. Top with an extra sprinkling of grated cheese. Season with salt and pepper.

4. Place the mushrooms, streaky bacon, cherry tomatoes, baked beans and the breakfast baguette onto a baking tray.

5. Drizzle olive oil over the ingredients and bake at 180°C for 8–10 minutes or until golden brown.

6. Slice the baguette and serve with the baked side dishes and avo slices.

BREAKFAST BITES | 37

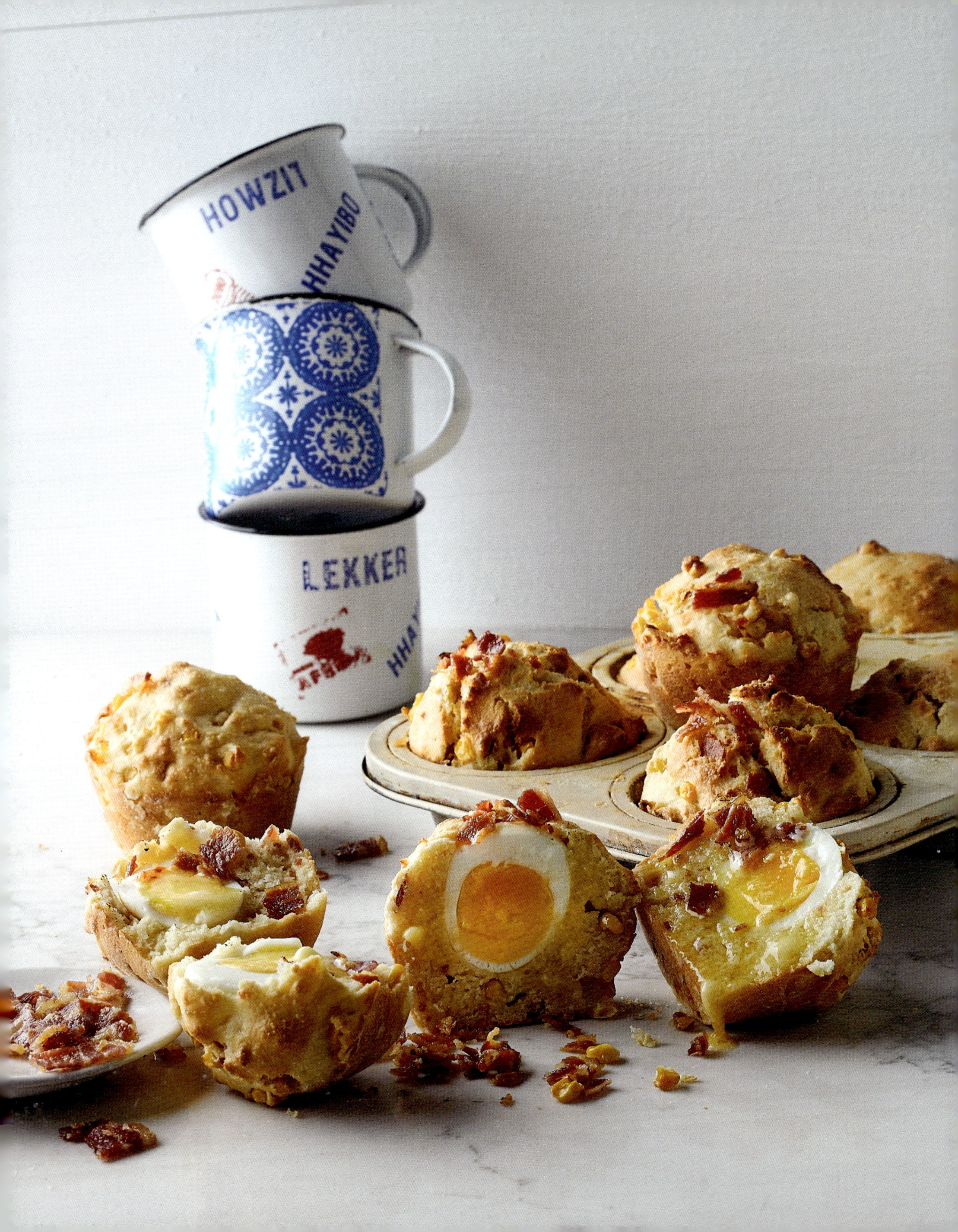
HOWZIT
HHAYIBO
LEKKER

MEALIE MEAL MUFFINS

Bet you've never tried an egg INSIDE a muffin before ...
top that with crispy bacon bits ... YUM!

10 eggs
2 packs (200 g each) streaky bacon
1¼ cups milk
¼ cup butter, melted
1½ cups White Star super maize meal
2½ cups flour
1½ tsp baking powder
1 tsp salt
1 can corn

1. Boil 6 eggs in a pot of boiling water for 5 minutes.

2. Once boiled, drain the water and replace it with cold water and cool for 5 minutes. Place the eggs in the fridge for 30 minutes before placing them in the freezer for 30 minutes.

3. Dice the bacon into bits, fry until cooked and set aside.

4. In a large mixing bowl, whisk the remaining 4 eggs, milk and melted butter.

5. In a separate bowl, combine maize meal, flour, baking powder and salt. Pour the liquid mixture into the bowl and whisk to combine. Once mixed, stir through the corn and the cooked bacon bits.

6. Rim a large 6-cup muffin tin with butter and flour.

7. Fill each cup of the muffin tin halfway with the mixture before placing a peeled boiled egg into the centre of each one. Fill each muffin cup with the remaining mixture, covering the eggs.

8. Bake for 20 minutes at 180°C, or until a skewer inserted in the centre comes out clean

9. Serve warm.

BREAKFAST PIZZA

An easy, fun and fruity no-bake breakfast pizza – kids especially, will love this one!

3 cups Food Lover's Market honey and almond muesli
½ cup Food Lover's Market almonds, chopped
½ tbsp Food Lover's Market cinnamon
1 cup Food Lover's Market smooth peanut butter
2 tbsp Food Lover's Market honey
1½ cups Food Lover's Market double cream yoghurt
Sliced fruit as preferred, e.g. naartjies, kiwis, banana, grapes

FOR SERVING
Handful chopped almonds
Honey

1. In a large mixing bowl, combine muesli, chopped almonds, cinnamon, peanut butter and honey.

2. Once mixed, spread the mixture onto a plate lined with a sheet of baking paper. This will help you to smooth the mixture into a pizza shape. Place in the freezer to set.

3. Once set, place the pizza base onto a chopping board and top with a layer of double cream yoghurt.

4. Using the fruit of your choosing, arrange fresh fruit slices on top of the base.

5. Top the fruit with a handful of chopped almonds and a drizzle of honey and serve.

You had me at 'pizza'!!!
– CHANTAL ANGELIQUE BEKKER

WHITE BEAN SHAKSHUKA

A family breakfast idea that's so full of flavour it will BLOW YOUR MIND!

1 cup IMBO white beans
2 tbsp olive oil for frying
1 onion, chopped
4 cloves garlic, crushed
1 can whole peeled tomatoes
½ tbsp paprika
1 tsp cumin
½ tsp dried oregano
½ tsp red pepper flakes
Salt and pepper
4 eggs
Feta, crumbled
Fresh parsley, chopped
Toasted ciabatta
Avocado slices

1. Boil the white beans for 5 minutes. Allow to soak for 1 hour once boiled.

2. Strain the beans and add fresh water to the pot before bringing to the boil, reducing the heat and allowing to simmer for 40–60 minutes.

3. Brown the onion and garlic in olive oil. Add the whole peeled tomatoes, paprika, cumin, dried oregano and red pepper flakes.

4. Season with salt and pepper and simmer while stirring the mixture.

5. Add the strained white beans.

6. Make four holes in the mixture and crack an egg into each.

7. Cover and simmer for 5 minutes or until the eggs are cooked.

8. Top with crumbled feta and chopped fresh parsley. Serve on toasted ciabatta with avocado slices.

BREAKFAST BITES | 41

PEANUT BUTTER CHOC POWER SMOOTHIE

A boost of flavour, fibre and energy to kick-start your day!

FOR THE SMOOTHIES
2 ripe large bananas, peeled, sliced and frozen
¼ cup smooth peanut butter
1 ½ cups milk of choice
1 cup ice
½ tsp vanilla essence
1 tbsp oats
½ cup Weet-Bix (2 blocks)
2 tbsp unsweetened cocoa powder

FOR THE GARNISH
2 tbsp peanut butter, melted
Roughly chopped nuts
1 banana (optional)

1. Chop the bananas and rim 2 smoothie jars with banana slices.

2. Place all smoothie ingredients except the cocoa powder into a blender and blend until smooth.

3. Pour two-thirds of this mixture into the jars until the banana slices are covered with the mixture.

4. Blend the remaining third of the mixture with cocoa powder and pour this into the jars.

5. For the garnish, heat the peanut butter in the microwave until a smoother consistency is achieved.

6. Top the smoothie with peanut butter and some roughly chopped nuts.

7. Serve with a banana straw made by skewering banana slices onto a paper straw.

I'm drooling looking at this. Can I order a take-away?
– CHEF MELISSA MAYO

LOVE IT!

SMOOTHIES FOUR WAYS:

Four creative recipes to mix up your smoothie routine!

BANANA AND STRAWBERRY LAVA SMOOTHIES

1 cup strawberries
½ cup light coconut milk
½ cup Greek yoghurt
½ tsp vanilla extract
½ pawpaw
1½ frozen bananas

1. Roughly chop the strawberries.

2. Blend the strawberries in a Nutribullet or a blender until smooth.

3. Pour the blended strawberries into the bottom of the glass.

4. Blend together the light coconut milk, Greek yoghurt, vanilla extract, pawpaw and frozen bananas until smooth.

5. Once smooth, pour the smoothie mixture over the blended strawberries and mix with a straw to create a lava effect.

6. Garnish with fresh strawberries and serve.

COCOA AND MINT BERRYLICIOUS BOWL

½ cup milk
½ tsp maple syrup
Fresh mint
½ ripe avocado
1 banana
1 tsp cocoa powder
Honey
Granola
Strawberry slices
Chia seeds
Cocoa nibs
Almonds

1. Blend the milk with maple syrup, fresh mint leaves, avocado, banana and cocoa powder.

2. Once smooth, pour into a bowl for serving.

3. Top with a drizzle of honey, granola, strawberry slices, chia seeds, cocoa nibs and almonds and serve.

SMOOTHIE SWIRL POPSICLES

1 cup strawberries
¾ cup blueberries
1 tsp honey
2 cups double cream yoghurt

1. Roughly chop the strawberries.
2. Blend the strawberries in a Nutribullet until smooth.
3. Blend the blueberries until smooth.
4. Add the honey to the double cream yoghurt and stir to combine.
5. In a popsicle mould, layer the double cream yoghurt mixture with alternating spoonfuls of the berry mixture.
6. Using a spoon, swirl the mixture before freezing.
7. Serve once frozen.

STRAWBERRY SMOOTHIE WITH CHIA SEED PUDDING

1 cup coconut milk
1 tbsp honey
3 tbsp chia seeds
1 cup frozen strawberries
1 frozen banana
2 dates
½ cup coconut water
Kiwi slices
Fresh strawberries
Coconut

1. Combine coconut milk with honey and chia seeds in a bowl. Refrigerate overnight.
2. Blend strawberries, banana, dates and coconut water until smooth.
3. Spoon the chia seed pudding into the bottom of the serving glasses, place kiwi slices on the sides of the glass before pouring the strawberry smoothie mixture over the chia seed pudding.
4. Garnish with slices of kiwi, fresh strawberries and coconut and serve.

FRUIT AND NUT YOGHURT BARS

A fun and fruity snack idea – so simple and so delicious!

Hazelnuts
2 cups strawberries – half with stem attached
3 cups double cream yoghurt
1 cup Ceres Secrets of the Valley fruit juice
2 cups blueberries
2 tbsp honey

1. Layer a square baking pan with baking paper.
2. The edges of the paper should stick out over the sides so that it can be removed easily once the yoghurt has set in the freezer.
3. Sprinkle hazelnuts over the baking pan.
4. Slice half of the strawberries (those with no stems).
5. In a medium-sized mixing bowl, combine the yoghurt, Ceres Secrets of the Valley fruit juice, sliced strawberries, half of the blueberries and honey. Stir to combine.
6. Pour the mixture into the baking pan and spread evenly.
7. Top with the remaining strawberries with stems intact and the remaining cup of blueberries.
8. Freeze for 4–6 hours. Lift the baking paper out of the pan and slice the set mixture into squares.
9. Serve immediately.

Looks so yummy!!!
– ISOLDE ZAGER ANDERSON

SUPER YUMMY BREAKFAST BARS

An on-the-go breakfast or snack option that the whole family will love!

3 cups Nature's Choice muesli
1 cup Safari raisins and cranberries
1 cup Safari roasted mixed nuts
80 g butter
200 g brown sugar
¼ cup honey
1 tsp Moir's vanilla essence
Chocolate

1. Place the muesli and the raisins and cranberries in a mixing bowl.

2. Roughly chop the roasted mixed nuts and add them to the mixing bowl.

3. Place the butter, brown sugar, honey and vanilla essence in a saucepan and allow to melt over low heat, stirring thoroughly.

4. Add the melted butter mixture to the mixing bowl and stir together until the muesli, dried fruit and nuts are coated.

5. Line a baking tray with baking paper and pour in the muesli mixture. Spread out the mixture evenly with a spatula. Place a second sheet of baking paper over the top and press down to compact and flatten the mixture.

6. Cover with foil and bake at 180°C for 15 minutes. Once baked, allow to cool.

7. Lift the baked mixture out of the baking tray using the baking paper and slice into even rectangular bars.

8. Melt some chocolate in a bowl over hot water. Once melted, drizzle the chocolate over the bars. Allow the chocolate to cool and harden before serving.

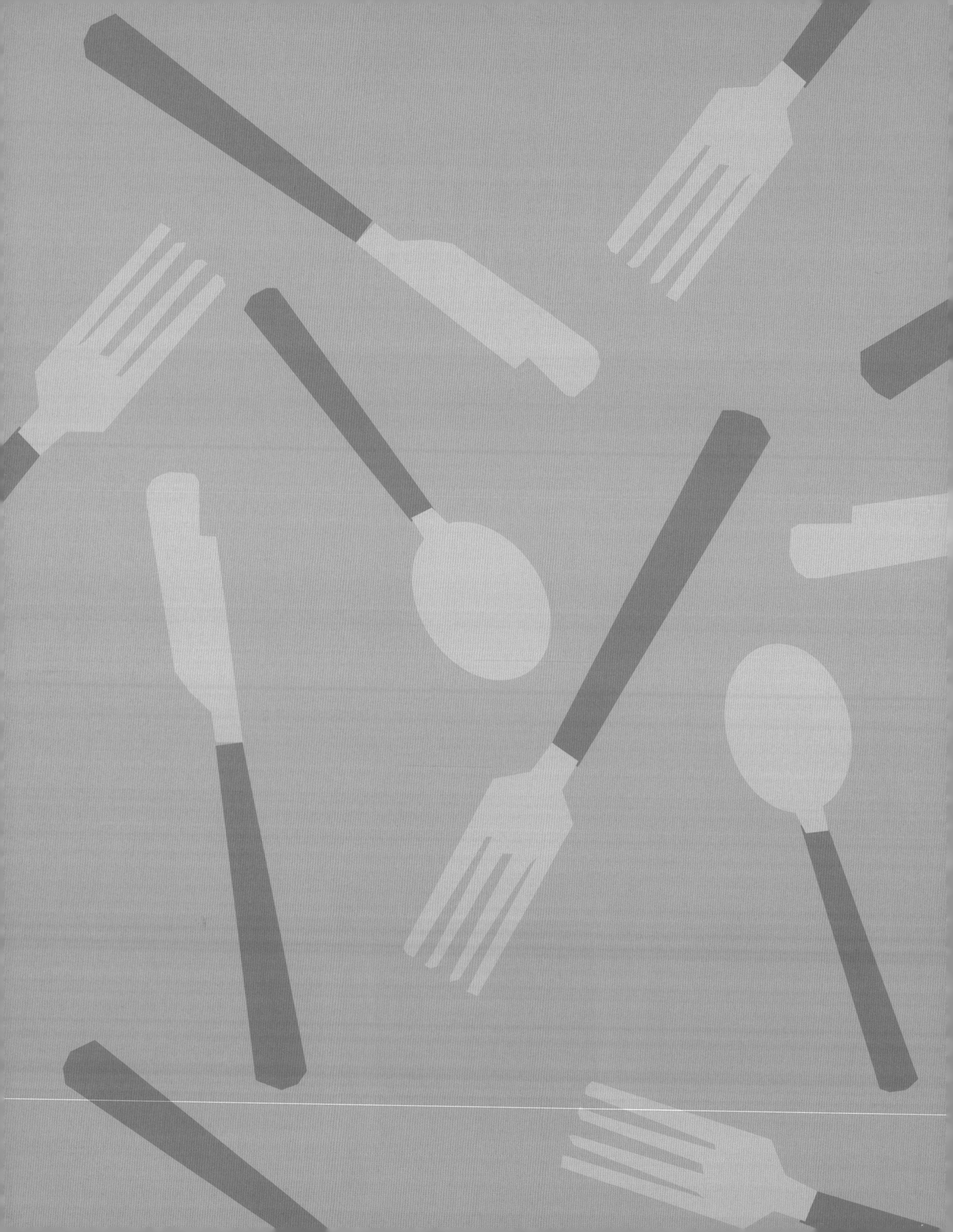

SAVOURY

QUICK BITES

EASY CAPRESE PASTRY SQUARES

Cherry tomatoes, basil pesto and melted mozzarella on a base of perfectly golden, flaky puff pastry...

1 sheet frozen puff pastry, thawed
½ cup basil pesto
1 pack (70 g) Galbani mozzarella
1 cup cherry tomatoes
½ tsp Italian seasoning, or more to taste
Salt to taste
Freshly ground black pepper
1 egg, whisked
1 tsp water
¼ cup fresh basil leaves, roughly torn

1. Make sure the frozen puff pastry is thawed before starting.

2. Preheat the oven to 200°C.

3. Prepare a baking sheet by lining it with baking paper.

4. Spread out the puff pastry on the tray and score the edge about 2 cm from the edge all the way around.

5. Spread the basil pesto evenly over the puff pastry.

6. Evenly place the mozzarella, roughly torn apart, over the basil pesto. Then add cherry tomatoes sliced in half.

7. Season with Italian seasoning and salt and freshly ground black pepper to taste. Make an egg wash by mixing the whisked egg with the water. Lightly brush over the edges of the puff pastry.

8. Bake for 6–8 minutes or until the puff pastry is light golden.

9. Be careful not to let the puff pastry burn.

10. Sprinkle with roughly torn fresh basil leaves.

11. Season to taste with more salt and pepper before slicing into squares and serving.

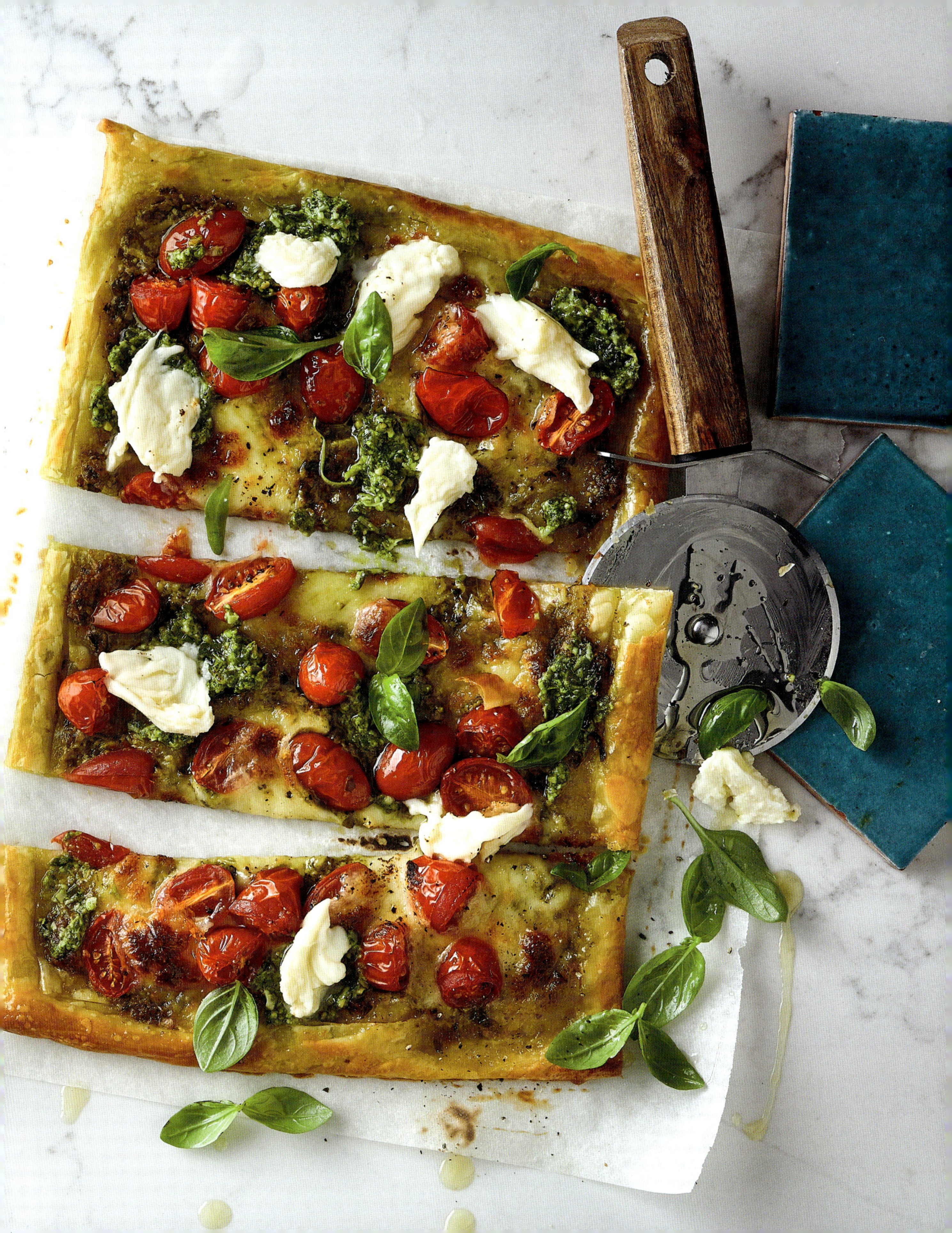

MUFFINS IN MUGS

*Great as a light lunch, an anytime snack or with your afternoon tea ...
(Warm from the oven with a smear of melting butter is best!)*

1 cup bacon bits
2 cups all-purpose flour
1 tbsp baking powder
¼ tsp bicarbonate of soda
½ tsp salt
¼ tsp dried oregano
2 eggs
¾ cup milk
½ cup melted President butter
2 tsp granulated sugar
2 cups packed baby spinach, roughly chopped
½ cup crumbled President feta cheese
Extra President feta for the garnish
Butter, for serving

1. Preheat the oven to 200°C.

2. Fry the bacon bits in a pan until golden and crispy. Set aside.

3. Whisk together the flour, baking powder, bicarbonate of soda, salt and oregano. Set aside.

4. In separate bowl, whisk together the eggs, milk, melted butter and sugar until blended. Stir the mixture into the dry ingredients until just combined (do not overmix). Fold in the spinach, ⅔ cup bacon bits and feta until just combined.

5. Spoon the muffin mixture into greased enamel mugs.

6. Sprinkle the remaining crispy bacon bits and feta over the muffins before baking.

7. Bake for 20–25 minutes.

8. Serve warm with butter.

GIANT CHEESE AND BOV(ROLL)

Bread dough + Bovril + butter + cheese = a GIANT CHEESE AND BOV(ROLL)!

1kg store-bought bread dough
4 tbsp Bovril
½ cup butter, softened
2 cups grated cheese
1 egg, for the egg wash
1 tsp water
Cream cheese
Chopped chives

1. Roll out the dough into a long rectangle (as thin as the dough will allow; roughly 30cm x 50cm.)

2. Mix the Bovril and butter together in a mixing bowl and set aside.

3. Top the pastry with the Bovril and butter mixture and spread.

4. Top with an even layer of grated cheese.

5. Gently press down the cheese so that it sticks to the dough.

6. Using a knife or a pizza cutter, cut the dough into strips, 2,5cm wide.

7. Roll the first piece into a 'wheel' or giant coil.

8. Join it to the next strip and continue rolling up the wheel from where the last piece of dough left off, until you've used up all the dough.

9. Spray a 24cm pie dish or quiche tin with non-stick spray.

10. Place the bread roll on the greased dish or tin and allow the dough to rise in a warm place for 30–45 minutes.

11. Preheat the oven to 180°C.

12. Whisk the egg and add a teaspoon of water if it is too thick. Brush the top of the risen roll with the egg wash and then bake in the oven for 20 minutes. (If it is getting too brown, cover the roll with foil, sprayed with oil so that it doesn't stick to the bread roll. You don't want it burning or getting too brown, as the cheese gets dry and crunchy.)

13. Bake for another 10 minutes and then remove from oven.

14. Slice and top with a dollop of cream cheese and some chives.

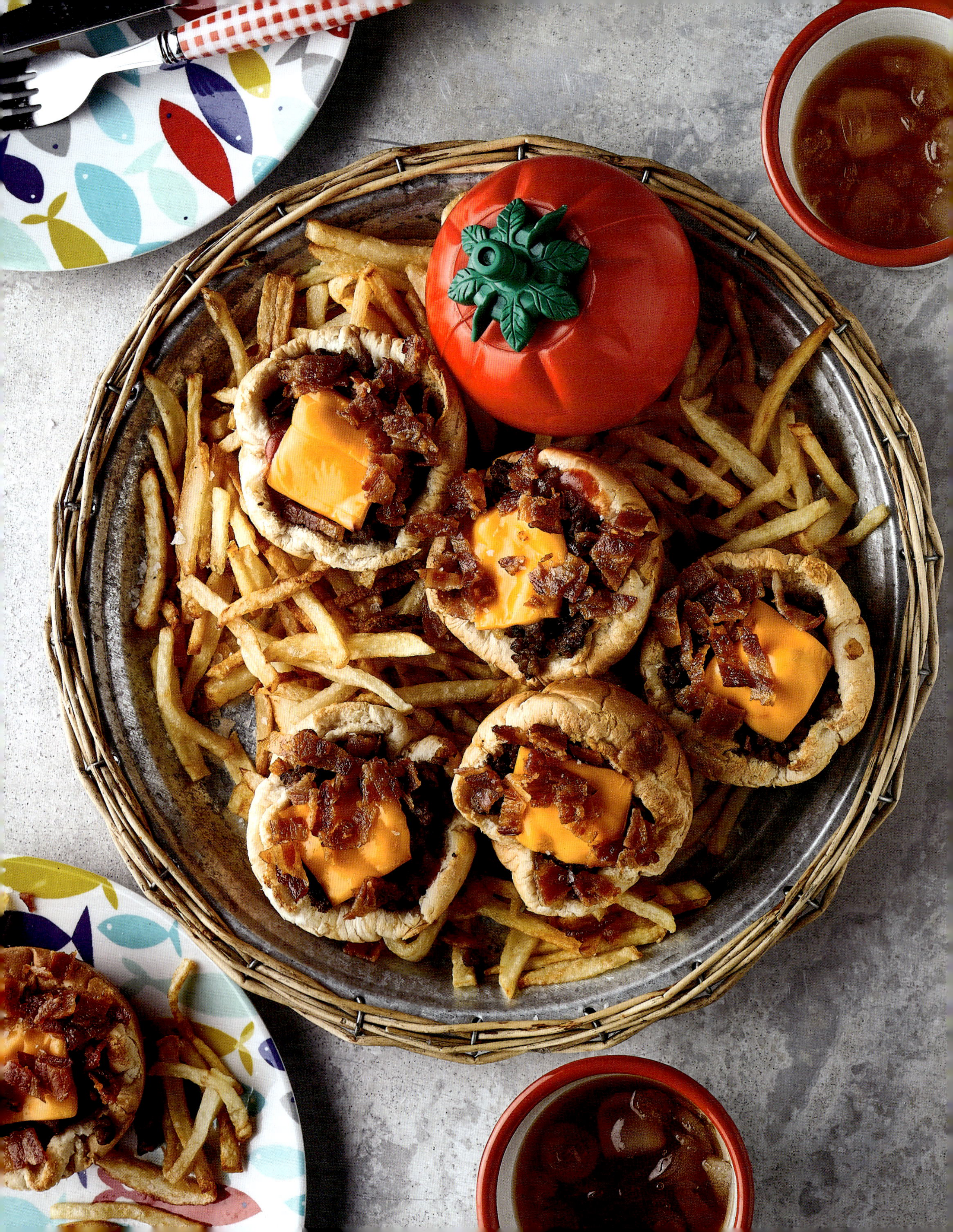

CHEESEBURGER BITES

Everything you love about cheeseburgers – in easy-to-make, easy-to-eat cup form ... sooo tasty!

1 tbsp President butter, melted
6 burger buns, cut in half
3 slices bacon, chopped
250 g beef mince
½ onion diced
½ tsp salt
Tomato sauce
3 slices Melrose melts, each cut into 4 squares
Gherkins, sliced

1. Preheat the oven to 180°C.

2. Brush the 12 cups of a regular-sized muffin tin with melted butter. Place half a bun, cut side up, into each muffin cup, and press it in to the edges. Set aside.

3. Meanwhile, cook bacon in a pan over over medium heat until crisp. Transfer to a paper towel-lined plate to drain. Pour off most of the fat but keep about a tablespoon in the pan for frying.

4. Add the mince, onion and salt to the pan. Cook for 5–7 minutes, stirring frequently, until the mince is brown and cooked through. Drain.

5. Divide the mixture evenly among the muffin cups. Gently press the mixture down into the cups. Top each with 1 teaspoon tomato sauce. Place a cheese square on top of each burger bite.

6. Bake for 7–9 minutes or until the cheese has melted. Immediately top with crispy cooked bacon, followed by gherkin slices and more tomato sauce if desired.

7. Serve with crispy skinny fries.

I used slices of bread and my children love it!
— **PEARL DU PLESSIS**

SAVOURY | 55

MAC 'N CHEESE BOERIE BITES

A soft, warm and yummy mac and cheese centre encased in a juicy meatball, served on a fresh, warm boerie roll ... comfort food on a whole new level!

500 g Fatti's & Moni's macaroni
2 tbsp butter
2 tbsp flour
2 cups milk
3 cups grated cheddar cheese
800 g mince
½ onion, finely chopped
¼ cup breadcrumbs
1 tbsp coriander seeds, crushed
¼ tsp nutmeg and cloves
1 tsp pepper
1 tsp salt
1 tbsp red wine vinegar
1 tbsp parsley
1 egg, beaten
Cheddar cheese cut into cubes
Non-stick cooking spray
BBQ basting sauce
Boerie rolls, warmed, for serving (use long or round rolls)

1. Boil the macaroni in lightly salted water until cooked, strain and set aside.

2. In a medium saucepan, melt the butter with the flour. Once combined pour in the milk. Stir continuously and allow to thicken.

3. Add the grated cheese to the mixture and stir to combine.

4. Combine the cheese sauce with the cooked macaroni.

5. In a large mixing bowl, combine the mince with onion, breadcrumbs, coriander seeds, nutmeg and cloves, pepper, salt, red wine vinegar, parsley and the beaten egg.

6. Mix until combined and form balls with the mixture. Flatten each ball and add a scoop of macaroni to the centre with one cube of cheddar cheese. Fold over and press to close. Spray an ovenproof dish or roasting pan with non-stick cooking spray and add the balls as you make them.

7. Baste the meatballs with BBQ sauce and bake for 20 minutes at 180°C.

8. Serve hot on warmed boerie rolls.

CRAN-BRIE BITES

Fun finger food, oozing with flavour ... Your family and friends will be blown away by this one!

FOR THE RICE BALLS
1 cup Tastic bonnet rice
3 cups water
1 egg
Salt and pepper
Brie cheese
Flour
1 egg, whisked
Breadcrumbs
Oil for frying

FOR THE SAUCE
350 g cranberries
1 cup orange juice
½ cup caster sugar
Orange zest

1. Bring the rice to the boil in lightly salted water. Simmer for 18–20 minutes until all the water has been absorbed and the rice grains are plump. Fluff apart with a fork. Set aside to cool before handling.

2. Once the rice has cooled, add the beaten egg and stir. Season with salt and pepper.

3. Slice the Brie cheese into cubes.

4. Spoon 1 tbsp of rice into your hand and flatten out the mixture.

5. Place one cube of Brie cheese in the centre and fold the sides to create a ball, enclosing the cheese in the centre.

6. Dip each ball in flour, egg and breadcrumbs before frying until golden and crispy.

7. Serve the cooked bites with the cranberry dipping sauce.

Cranberry suace

1. In a separate pan, heat the cranberries with orange juice, caster sugar and orange zest.

2. Bring to the boil and simmer the mixture until it achieves a syrupy consistency.

CHAKALAKA BREAD

Wow! Now these are seriously NEXT LEVEL braaibroodjies!

1 cup White Star super maize meal
2 cups all-purpose flour
1 tbsp baking powder
3 tbsp chopped spring onion
salt and pepper to taste
1 tbsp sugar
¼ cup olive oil
2 tbsp plain yoghurt
3 eggs
1 can corn
1 can chakalaka
1 cup grated cheese
4 empty, clean cans
Butter and flour to coat the cans

1. In a large mixing bowl, combine the maize meal, flour, baking powder, spring onion, salt, pepper, sugar, olive oil, yoghurt, eggs and corn.

2. Mix to create a dough-like consistency. Spread flour over your working area before rolling out the dough using a rolling pin.

3. Spread the chakalaka over the flattened bread dough. Top with grated cheese.

4. Roll up the bread dough into one long log. Cut the dough into 4 lengths measuring roughly 10cm. Place the dough sections into the 4 cans, which have been coated with butter and flour.

5. Bake for 30 minutes at 180°C.

6. Remove the chakalaka bread from the cans and serve.

Wow, I'm definitely gonna try this bread!
– NTOMBI DLAMINI

CHAKA-LEKKA!

BILTONG AND CHEESE ROLL-UPS

Biltong + cheese + crispy garlic toast = a super simple and delicious snack idea that takes mere minutes to make!

8 slices of Sasko premium white bread
Cheddar cheese, cut into strips
1 cup biltong shavings
Fresh parsley
1 tsp crushed garlic
Salt and pepper to taste
3 tbsp butter, melted
Tomato sauce for dipping (or other dipping sauce of your choice)

1. Cut the crusts off the bread slices.
2. Cut the cheese into strips measuring roughly the same length as each bread slice.
3. Place the bread slices on a tray. Sprinkle the biltong shavings evenly over each bread slice.
4. Place a strip of cheddar cheese in the centre of each bread slice.
5. Roll up each bread slice and press the edges together so that the cheese and biltong shavings are held tightly in the centre of the bread.
6. Finely dice some fresh parsley.
7. Add the parsley, crushed garlic and salt and pepper to the melted butter and mix to combine.
8. Using a pastry brush, brush the bread parcels with the garlic butter.
9. Bake for 10 minutes at 180°C or until golden and toasted.
10. Serve with tomato sauce for dipping.

I made this today – yum!
– MAPHATHE MPHO

CHEESY BREAD BOAT

CHEESE ×3 + bread + wine = a creamy, dreamy, DELICIOUS snack idea!

1 large Italian loaf
1 cup President cream cheese
⅘ cup white wine
2 tbsp all-purpose flour
2 tbsp lemon juice
Salt to taste
1 cup grated Parmalat cheddar cheese
¼ cup fresh mixed herbs
½ tsp crushed garlic
A dash of olive oil
1 round of President Camembert cheese

1. Cut out the top of the bread to create a bowl shape. Hollow out any extra bread inside to define the bowl shape. Slice the top of the bread into strips for dipping.

2. Place the cream cheese in a mixing bowl with the wine, flour and lemon juice. Add salt to taste.

3. Add the grated cheddar cheese to the mixture.

4. Place the bread on a baking sheet and fill it with the cheese mixture. Place the bread slices next to the bread boat.

5. Chop the fresh herbs and mix together the herbs, garlic and olive oil.

6. Spoon the herb mixture over the chopped bread slices.

7. Place a round of Camembert into the middle of the cheese-filled bread boat.

8. Bake for 20–30 minutes at 180°C.

9. Once out of the oven, use a sharp knife to cut a cross in the top of the Camembert to reveal the melted cheese inside.

10. Serve with the toasted herb and garlic bread dippers.

Staaaaaaaaapppppp!!!
❤️🤪🤪🤪
– LORNA MASEKO

CHEESY SAGO POPPERS

Ever tried sago before? If not, you HAVE to try these gluten-free poppers!

1 cup Imbo sago pearls
2 medium-sized potatoes
¼ cup Imbo desiccated coconut
2 eggs
1 tsp chilli powder
½ tsp dried coriander powder
1 cup fresh parsley leaves, finely chopped
Salt to taste
1 cup flour
200 g cheese, cut into blocks
Oil for frying
Parmesan cheese, to top

1. Soak the sago pearls for 1 hour, strain and set aside.

2. Microwave the potatoes for 10 minutes. Allow them to cool slightly before peeling and then mashing them.

3. Combine the mashed potato with the desiccated coconut, eggs, chilli powder, dried coriander and fresh parsley.

4. Mix through the sago and season the mixture with salt to taste. Add flour until the mixture holds together to form balls.

5. Scoop out balls of the mixture, flatten them out and add a block of cheese to each ball for a cheesy centre.

6. Fry the balls in oil until golden brown and allow to cool on a sheet of kitchen towel to drain excess oil.

7. Top with parmesan cheese, skewer and serve.

CHEESY 😀

BIRYANI BOMBS

Perfectly crisp on the outside, with a fluffy and fragrant filling, these Biryani Bombs are a fun way to mix up your next curry night!

1 cup Aunt Caroline parboiled rice
¼ cup flour
¼ cup cornflour
½ cup water
½ cup mixed frozen vegetables
2 tbsp oil
¼ cup onion, diced
2 tsp ginger
¼ cup tomato, diced
1 ½ tsp biryani masala
½ tsp chilli powder
½ cup cottage cheese
¼ cup fresh coriander, chopped
Breadcrumbs
Oil for frying

FOR THE YOGHURT AND CORIANDER DIPPING SAUCE

1 cup plain yoghurt of your choice
Small handful fresh coriander, chopped (or more to taste)
Salt and freshly ground pepper
Chopped fresh chilli (optional)

1. Bring the rice to the boil in lightly salted water, allow to simmer until cooked. Allow to cool.

2. In a small bowl, whisk the flour with the cornflour and water. Set aside.

3. In a small pan, bring the mixed frozen vegetables to the boil and simmer until cooked. Strain and set aside.

4. Heat the 2 tablespoons of oil in a pan, brown the diced onion with ginger, diced tomato, biryani masala and chilli powder. Add in the mixed veggies and cottage cheese and stir to combine.

5. Add the rice and chopped coriander to the mixture and mix thoroughly.

6. Roll the mixture into balls measuring roughly 1 tablespoon each.

7. Dip each ball in the flour mixture and breadcrumbs before frying until golden brown.

8. For the dipping sauce, mix together the yoghurt, chopped fresh coriander and salt and pepper to taste. Add a chopped fresh chilli or chillies if desired.

When food is life ...
– AVISHA SITHALPARSAD

CHEESY MAIZE BITES

These proudly South African cheesy mealie meal bites are A-MAIZE-BALLS ... and a great snack option at a braai, picnic or party.

2 cups water
1 cup cream
Salt to taste
1½ cups White Star super maize meal
Olive oil for frying
1 onion, diced
1 clove garlic, crushed
1 cup grated cheddar cheese
½ cup biltong shavings
½ tsp ground nutmeg
Salt and pepper to taste
16 cubes of cheddar cheese (roughly 1 x 1 cm)
½ cup flour
3 eggs, beaten
Oil for frying
Chutney, to serve

1. Heat the water, add the cream and salt to taste.

2. Add 1 cup maize meal to the pot and cook for 5 minutes, stirring continuously. Remove from the heat and allow to cool.

3. Heat olive oil in a separate pan and brown diced onion and crushed garlic.

4. Place the cooked maize meal in a large mixing bowl, add the grated cheese, biltong shavings, nutmeg, salt and pepper. Mix and once combined, add the browned onions and garlic to the maize meal mixture.

5. Form the mixture into balls and pop a cube of cheese into each ball. Coat each ball in flour, egg and the remaining maize meal. Repeat the egg and maize meal step twice.

6. Fry until golden and crispy and serve with a chutney dipping sauce.

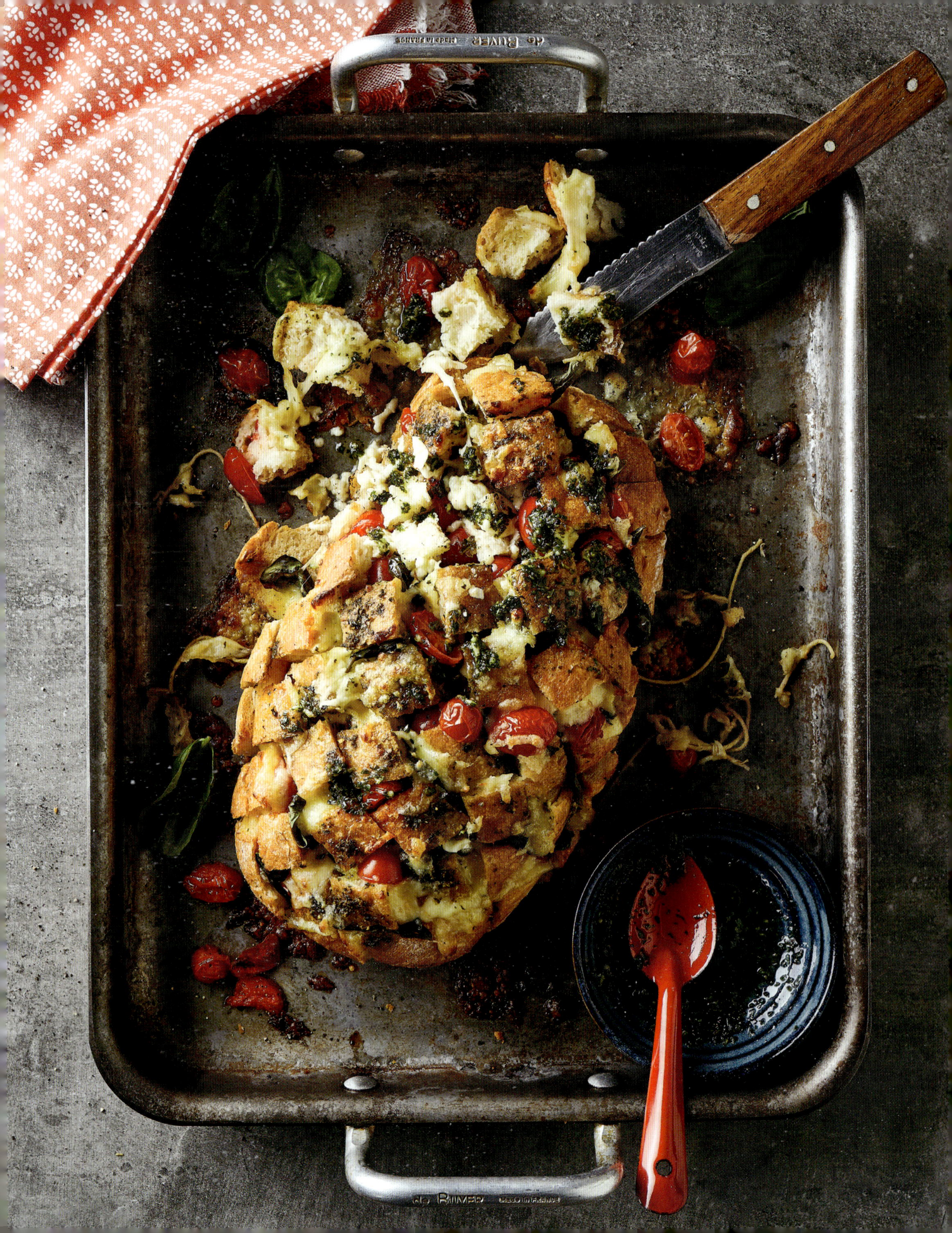

CAPRESE PULL-APART BREAD

A super simple snack idea that tastes even better than it looks!

1 large ciabatta loaf
½ cup basil leaves
2 tbsp crushed garlic
⅔ cup olive oil
2 packs (70 g each) Galbani mozzarella
1 cup rosa tomatoes
Handful fresh basil leaves

OMG!
– RHODA BLACKWELL

1. Cut the ciabatta loaf diagonally to form diamond shapes, making sure not to cut all the way down to the base of the bread.

2. Blend ½ cup basil leaves with the crushed garlic and olive oil. When blended, use a brush to coat the insides and top of the loaf with the basil oil.

3. Slice one pack of mozzarella into strips and place these into the cuts in the ciabatta, making sure to fill the gaps.

4. Chop rosa tomatoes in half and place these into the cuts in the loaf with the mozzarella.

5. Fill the remaining gaps with basil leaves.

6. Grate the other pack of mozzarella and sprinkle the grated cheese over the loaf before baking at 200°C for 15–20 minutes or until the cheese is golden.

7. Serve on a platter with a selection of cold meats and tasty finger treats.

CALZONE DIPPERS

Three epic pizza-style dippers made with minimal fuss and maximum flavour.

FOR THE REGINA CALZONE
3 slices Sasko Premium white bread
3 tbsp marinara sauce
⅓ cup grated mozzarella cheese,
⅓ cup ham, cut into strips
⅓ cup mushrooms, chopped

FOR THE MARGARITA CALZONE
3 slices Sasko Premium white bread
3 tbsp marinara sauce
⅓ cup grated mozzarella cheese
Basil leaves

FOR THE HAWAIIAN CALZONE
3 slices Sasko Premium white bread
3 tbsp marinara sauce
⅓ cup grated mozzarella cheese
⅓ cup ham, cut into strips
⅓ cup pineapple, chopped

1 egg, beaten
Oregano
Parmesan cheese, grated
Marinara sauce, for dipping

1. Cut the crusts off the 9 slices of bread (be careful not to cut too much bread away).

2. Preheat the oven to 180°C.

3. Place the bread slices on a greased baking tray in rows of three.

4. In the middle of each slice of bread in the first row, place a portion of the marinara sauce, grated cheese, ham strips, and chopped mushrooms.

5. In the middle of each slice of bread in the second row, place a portion of marinara sauce, grated cheese and basil leaves.

6. In the middle of each slice of bread in the third row, place a portion of the marinara sauce, grated cheese, ham strips and pineapple pieces.

7. Brush the edges with egg wash and fold each of the bread slices over into a triangle. Use a fork to press along the edges of the triangle to seal it closed.

8. Brush the top of each calzone with the beaten egg. Then sprinkle with oregano.

9. Place in the oven and bake for 10–12 minutes, or until the tops are golden brown.

10. Sprinkle with grated parmesan cheese and serve warm with extra marinara sauce for dipping.

BUTTER CHICKEN PASTRY PARCELS

These crispy, golden triangles are elegant and easy to make – an impressive snack for your next dinner party!

FOR THE PASTRY PARCELS
Oil for frying
3 chicken breast fillets, butterflied
2 garlic cloves, finely chopped
Fresh chilli (optional)
1 onion, chopped
400 g Royco Butter Chicken Cook-in-Sauce
Handful of fresh coriander
1 box of phyllo pastry
1 egg, beaten
3 tsp milk
Salt
Flaked almonds
Chopped fresh coriander

FOR THE DIPPING SAUCE
1 cup plain yoghurt
1 small cucumber, grated
2 garlic cloves, chopped
1 tbsp lemon juice
1 tbsp chutney
Salt to taste

1. Heat some oil in a pan and gently fry the chicken breast fillets until cooked through. Remove from the pan and, once cooled, shred with a fork.

2. Add the garlic, chilli (optional) and the onion to the same pan and fry until brown.

3. Add the butter chicken cook-in-sauce and the shredded chicken. Simmer for about 10 minutes.

4. Roughly chop the coriander and stir through before removing from heat and allowing to cool – the flavour will develop and the sauce will thicken slightly.

5. Cut each pastry sheet into about 5 strips. Once the chicken mixture has cooled, spoon roughly 1 tbsp of butter chicken onto one end of your pastry strip and fold diagonally into a triangle shape. Keep folding across and seal with beaten egg.

6. Brush the pastry triangles with a simple egg mix made with remaining egg, the milk and a pinch of salt. Sprinkle with flaked almonds.

7. Pop these almond-crusted pies into the oven at 180°C and bake for 10–15 minutes or until golden brown.

8. Prepare the dipping sauce using plain yoghurt, grated cucumber, chopped garlic cloves, lemon juice, chutney and salt.

9. Garnish with fresh coriander and serve.

SPICY BEAN DIP

It's hard to believe that something so tasty is so healthy and easy to make!

1 cup Imbo red speckled beans
1 cup Imbo kidney beans
1 cup Imbo small white beans
½ cup sour cream
Fresh coriander
1 clove garlic
Chilli
3 tbsp olive oil
Juice of 1 lemon
Salt
Pepper
Micro vegetables (optional)
Mixed seeds (optional)

1. In a large bowl, soak the red speckled beans, kidney beans and small white beans overnight.

2. Drain the soaked beans, cover them with fresh water and bring them to the boil in a large saucepan.

3. Reduce the heat and simmer for 1 hour or until soft.

4. Drain and pour the cooked beans into a blender, adding the sour cream, fresh coriander, garlic, chilli, olive oil, lemon juice, salt and pepper.

5. Blend until smooth.

6. To serve the bean dip, line a small terracotta pot with aluminium foil and spoon in the bean dip mixture.

7. Top the dip with micro vegetables and mixed seeds to create a mini garden.

> What a presentation! I spent 30 minutes taking pictures before eating this. LOL!
> – SIZWE NDLAZI

SAVOURY

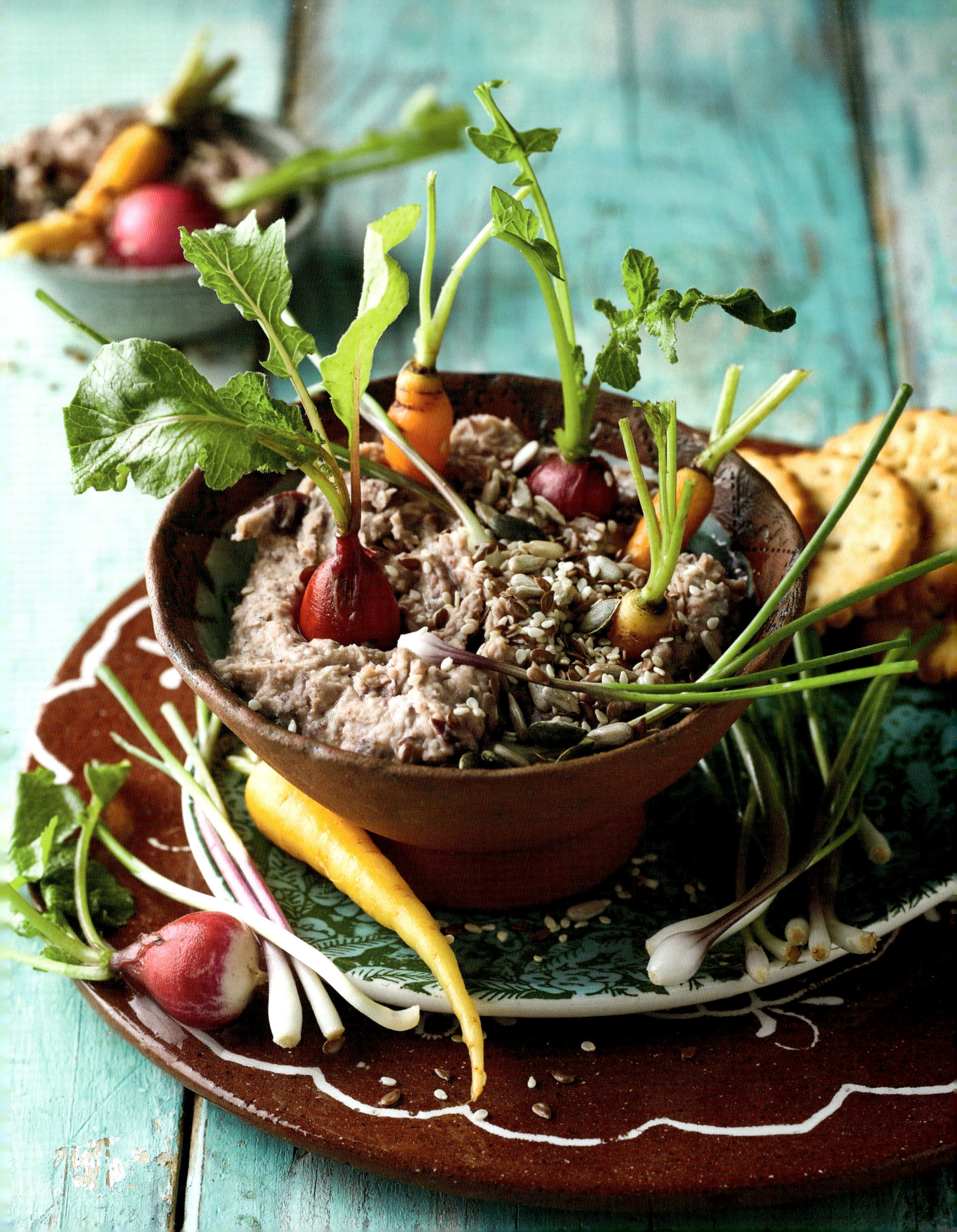

A-MAIZE-ZING CHAKALAKA DIPPERS

Pap + chakalaka + cheese = a scrumptious snack idea for your next braai!

6 cups water
2 tsp salt
2 tbsp butter
3 cups White Star super maize meal
1 cup chakalaka
1 cup grated cheddar cheese
1 cup flour
1 egg, beaten
Extra maize meal, for dipping
Oil for frying
Chakalaka, for dipping
Chutney, for dipping

1. Pour the water into a large pot, add the salt and butter and bring to the boil.

2. Slowly pour the maize meal into the pot to form a cone in the centre but don't stir. Cover with a lid, reduce the heat to low and allow the pap to simmer for 40 minutes.

3. Once cooked, set the pap aside and allow it to cool completely.

4. Form about 1 cup of pap into a stick shape, flatten out the pap and place a spoonful of chakalaka in the centre with grated cheese. Fold over the pap and press the stick closed.

5. Repeat the process with all the pap.

6. Dip each maize meal stick in flour, beaten egg and maize meal. Repeat the process again before frying the sticks in oil until golden and crispy.

7. Serve with chakalaka and chutney for dipping.

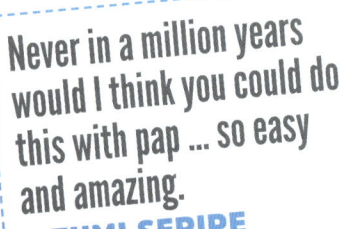

> Never in a million years would I think you could do this with pap ... so easy and amazing.
> — TUMI SERIPE

CHEESY RICE SNACKS

Bite-sized balls and cheese biltong sticks oozing with melted mozzarella ... YUM!

1½ cups Tastic parboiled rice
4½ cups water
1 tsp salt
1 cup grated mozzarella
4 eggs
Salt and pepper to taste
1½ tbsp Mrs Ball's chutney
1½ tbsp biltong shavings
4 small cubes mozzarella
4 small strips of mozzarella
1 cup flour
1 cup breadcrumbs
Oil for frying
Dipping sauces, to serve

1. Bring the rice to the boil in lightly salted water. Reduce to a simmer and cook for 25–30 minutes. Once cooked, drain the rice.

2. Once cooked, combine the rice, grated mozzarella and 3 eggs in a large bowl, season with salt and pepper. Use your hands to thoroughly combine the mixture.

3. Divide the mixture into two equal portions in two bowls.

4. Add the chutney to the first bowl for the balls, stir to combine.

5. Add the biltong shavings to the second bowl for the cheesy biltong sticks, stir to combine.

6. If the mixture is a little too wet, add a few teaspoons of flour.

7. Form each ball by taking a small portion of the mixture from the first bowl, rolling it into a ball, squeezing it firmly and stuffing one cube of cheese inside each ball. Repeat to make 3 more balls.

8. Roll the mixture from the second bowl into 4 stick shapes, place a strip of cheese into each, fold over and seal the stick shape firmly.

9. Whisk the remaining egg in a bowl.

10. Dip each ball and stick in flour, egg and then in the breadcrumbs, shaking off any excess. Repeat the process once more.

11. Fry in oil until golden brown and cooked through. Serve with a selection of dipping sauces.

MAINS

CHICKEN AND BROCCOLI PUFF PASTRY RING

A ring of puff pastry with a flavour-packed chicken/broccoli filling – a guaranteed crowd pleaser!

1 tbsp olive oil
2 cups chicken breast meat, cubed
2 tbsp milk
1 cup cream cheese, softened
1 sachet Knorr Naturally Tasty Creamy Chicken and Broccoli Bake
Salt and pepper to taste
1 tsp garlic powder
1 cup broccoli, lightly steamed
1 packet puff pastry
1 egg, beaten

NOTE: Check out the recipe video on Facebook or Instagram to see how the puff pastry should be cut and placed on the baking tray.

1. Heat olive oil in a pan, fry the chicken pieces for a few minutes. Stir the milk through until browned.

2. In a bowl, mix the cream cheese and the contents of the sachet. Season with salt and pepper and add garlic powder.

3. Add the cooked chicken to the cream cheese mixture together with lightly steamed broccoli.

4. Roll out the puff pastry using a rolling pin and flour.

5. Using a pizza cutter, slice the puff pastry dough into 8 evenly-shaped triangles.

6. On a greased baking tray, place the triangular pieces in a circle so that the wide side of each triangle overlaps slightly to make a circle and the pointed sides point out.

7. Using a fork, press down on the overlapping sides to pinch them together.

8. Scoop the chicken and broccoli mixture evenly around the circle, then pull the points of the triangles gently over the top of the mixture to secure the ring.

9. Brush with beaten egg. Bake at 180°C for 20 minutes or until the puff pastry ring is lightly browned and golden.

10. Slice and serve.

SAVOURY

WICKED!

MEATBALL LASAGNE SOUP

Home-made meatballs smothered in a rich bolognaise sauce, topped with lasagne noodles and of course ... CHEESE!!

FOR THE MEATBALLS
300 g beef mince
1 small onion, finely diced
2 cloves garlic, grated
1 egg, lightly beaten
½ cup breadcrumbs
2 tbsp parsley and/or basil, chopped
Salt and pepper to taste
Oil for frying

FOR THE SOUP
1 tbsp oil
1 onion, chopped
2 stalks celery, diced
2 carrots, peeled and diced
4 cloves garlic, crushed
1 small can tomato paste
1⅕ cups chicken stock
Royco Bolognaise Cook-in-Sauce
5 lasagne sheets, broken into pieces
Grated mozzarella

1. Mix together all the meatball ingredients. Roll them into 1–2 tablespoon-sized balls and pan fry in oil over medium heat until browned on all sides, 2–4 minutes per side.

2. Heat oil in an ovenproof pot over medium-high heat. Add onions, celery and carrots and cook until tender, 5–10 minutes.

3. Add the garlic and fry for 1 minute, or until fragrant. Add the tomato paste and fry for a few minutes.

4. Add the chicken stock, the cook-in-sauce, meatballs and lasagne noodles (broken into small rough squares 3cm x 3cm) and bring to the boil. Reduce the heat to a simmer. Simmer for about 10 minutes or until the pasta is tender.

5. Top with a generous amount of grated mozzarella and bake in the oven until the cheese is melted and golden.

6. Serve with garlicky bruschetta toast.

LOADED CRUSTLESS QUICHE

A veggie-friendly, high-protein meal that you can whip up in minutes!

8 eggs
½ cup milk
Salt and pepper to taste
3 tbsp olive oil
1 onion, chopped
1 cup cherry tomatoes, halved
1 cup mushrooms, sliced
2 handfuls baby spinach
1 tsp dried oregano
100 g President feta cheese, broken into chunks
Cherry tomatoes on the vine
A little extra crumbled President feta for serving
Fresh basil for serving

1. Preheat the oven to 200°C.

2. Into a bowl, crack the eggs and add the milk, season with salt and pepper and whisk thoroughly. Set aside.

3. Add the oil to an ovenproof pan (preferably a cast-iron skillet) and add the onion. Sauté for 4 minutes until the onions are translucent.

4. Add the halved cherry tomatoes and mushrooms and fry for a few minutes until soft.

5. Add the spinach and stir until it begins to wilt.

6. Sprinkle over the oregano. Then pour in the egg mixture.

7. Break the feta cheese chunks evenly on top and place the vine cherry tomatoes in the centre.

8. Cook for just 2–3 minutes till the bottom begins to set. Then transfer the skillet to the preheated oven.

9. Cook for 15–20 minutes until just set. Turn on the grill of the oven to brown the top for about 5 minutes.

10. Serve hot or at room temperature sprinkled with salt and pepper, more crumbled feta and fresh basil.

MUFFIN TIN CHICKEN PIES

These family- and freezer-friendly home-made chicken pies are the PERFECT make-ahead dinner option for busy weeknights ... Students, parents and professionals – this one is for you!

- 2 large chicken breast fillets, cubed
- ¾ cup carrots, chopped
- ¾ cup mushrooms, chopped
- ¼ cup green beans, chopped
- ¾ cup celery, chopped
- 2 Knorr chicken stock pots
- ⅓ cup butter
- ⅓ cup onion, chopped
- ⅓ cup flour
- ½ tbsp Robertsons garlic salt
- ¼ tsp Robertsons black pepper
- 1 cup milk
- 2 packs puff pastry

Note: For convenience's sake, you could also freeze the completely-cooled pies after baking them.

1. Add the chicken to a pot together with the carrots, mushrooms, green beans and celery. Add enough water to cover the ingredients and add the Knorr chicken stock pots, keeping a little aside for brushing on the pie lids in 9, below.

2. Boil for 15 minutes before draining the chicken stock into a bowl and setting the chicken and vegetables aside.

3. In a frying pan, melt the butter and add the chopped onion. Add the flour, garlic salt and black pepper. Slowly pour in 1 ¾ cups of the chicken stock and the milk, all the while stirring continuously.

4. Simmer the sauce until it is thickened.

5. Grease a large 6-cup muffin tin (or use individual ramekins). Roll out the puff pastry using a rolling pin and flour. Cut out circles from the dough, rolling out each one until it is big enough to be pressed into a muffin tin cup with an overhang of 1,5 cm.

6. Use an empty, clean can to cut out the pie lids. You'll need 6 pie lids.

7. Combine the cooked chicken and vegetables with the sauce for the pie filling.

8. Spoon the filling into each pie case and close the pies with the lids, making sure to seal the edges by pinching them together. (Note: If freezing the pies, do so at this stage for best results, but allow the filling to cool completely before adding it to the pastry casings.)

9. Brush the pie lids with Knorr chicken stock from a stock pot and bake for 30 minutes at 180°C until golden brown.

10. Serve warm.

SO TASTY!

CHICKEN AND BARLEY BAKE

A wholesome weeknight dinner option, all cooked in one pot to reduce dishes!

6 chicken thighs
Olive oil
1 cup mushrooms
1 cup onion, chopped
Crushed garlic to taste
2 ½ cups chicken stock
1 ½ cups boiling water
1 cup white wine
1 cup Imbo pearl barley
Salt to taste
2 tbsp fresh thyme
1 ½ cups cooked garden peas

1. Fry the chicken thighs in olive oil on both sides until a deep golden brown.

2. Remove the chicken from the pan and add the mushrooms, onion and crushed garlic. Brown for 5 minutes.

3. Add the chicken stock, boiling water, white wine and pearl barley to the pot. Season with salt.

4. Add fresh thyme and bring to the boil before adding the chicken thighs back into the pot.

5. Simmer for 45 minutes.

6. Remove the chicken thighs from the pot.

7. Stir through cooked garden peas and serve the chicken thighs on top of the barley mixture.

Adding some curry or chillies for those cold winter nights will be good.
– KAREN SWEETNAM

SHREDDED CHICKEN
TACOS

Perfectly tender chicken, shredded and served in crisp taco shells,
topped with melted cheese and healthy trimmings.

4 skinless chicken breast fillets
1 packet taco seasoning
2 limes
1 can chopped tomatoes
⅓ cup chopped coriander
Robertsons Atlantic sea salt
Robertsons black pepper
1 Knorr chicken stock pot
6 taco shells
1 cup grated mozzarella cheese
½ cup sour cream
1 fresh tomato, diced
1 avocado, diced
1 cup shredded cabbage
Lime juice for drizzling

1. Place the chicken breast fillets into a pot topped with taco seasoning, the juice from the limes, chopped tomatoes, coriander, salt, pepper and chicken stock pot.

2. Cook for 90 minutes on medium heat.

3. Once cooked, shred the cooked chicken with a fork and top with the remaining sauce from the pot.

4. Stack taco shells in a baking dish to keep them upright and spoon a generous helping of chicken into each taco. Sprinkle grated cheese over the tacos.

5. Bake at 180°C until the cheese has melted and is golden.

6. Add a spoonful of sour cream to each taco followed by diced tomato, diced avocado and shredded cabbage.

7. Finish with a drizzle of lime juice and serve.

SAVOURY | 81

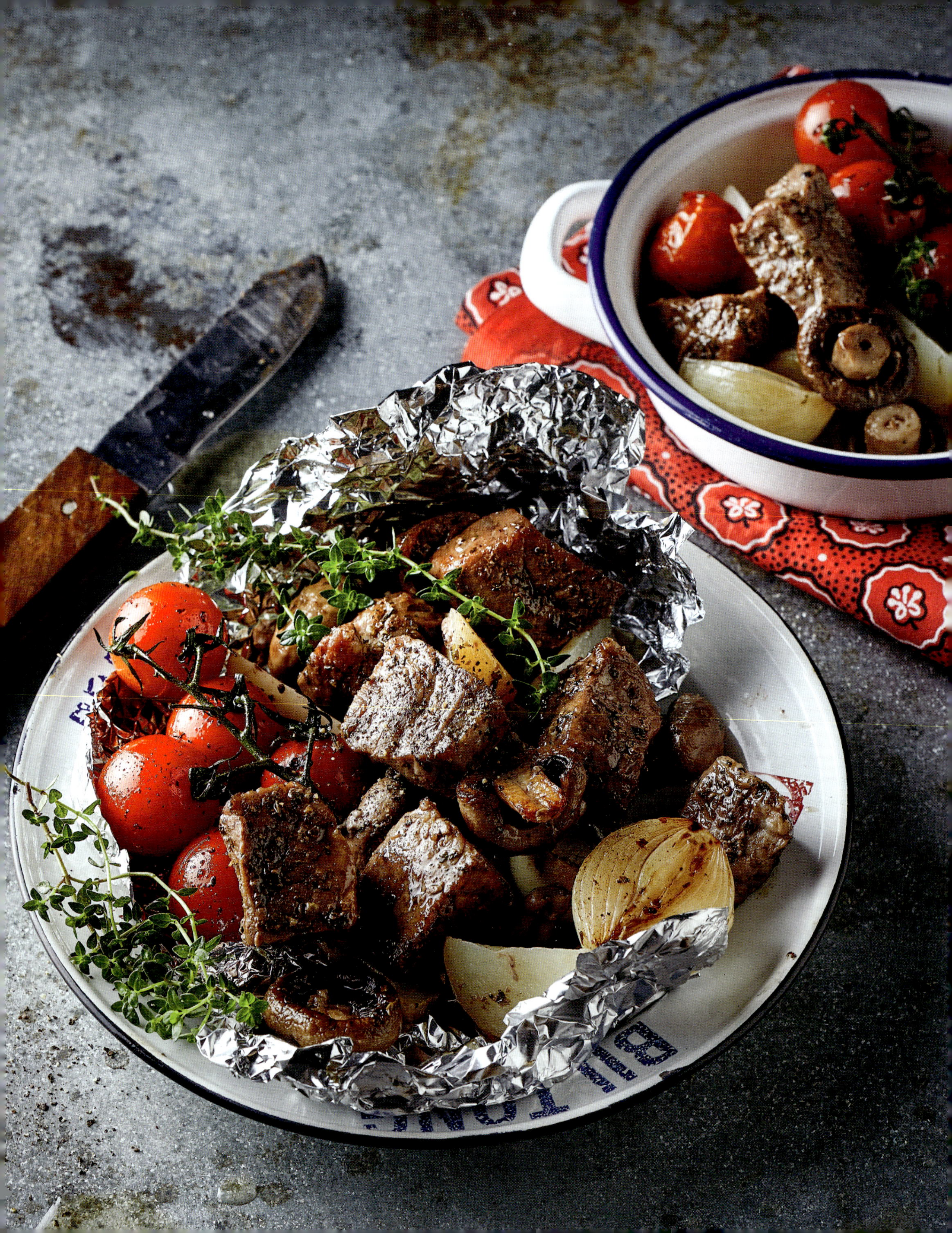

GARLIC STEAK FOIL PACK

A super simple, super tasty weeknight dinner option that takes minimal effort to prepare and requires practically no cleanup.

- 450 g Food Lover's Market Karan beef sirloin steak, trimmed of fat
- 8 Food Lover's Market potjie potatoes
- 6 baby onions
- 1 cup button mushrooms
- 1 tbsp Food Lover's Market crushed garlic
- 1 tsp Food Lover's Market dried parsley
- 1 tsp Food Lover's Market dried origanum
- Salt and pepper to taste
- 3 tbsp B-well blended canola and olive oil
- Baby tomatoes on the vine
- Fresh thyme

1. Slice the steak or cut it into chunks. Cut the potatoes into quarters or wedges. Halve the baby onions. Also halve the mushrooms if you wish.

2. In a large bowl, combine the steak, potatoes, baby onions, mushrooms, crushed garlic, parsley, origanum, salt, pepper and oil. Toss to combine.

3. Cut a large sheet of heavy-duty aluminium into a square measuring roughly 30 x 30 cm.

4. Place the seasoned mixture onto the sheet of foil, topped with baby tomatoes on a vine and fresh thyme.

5. Wrap the foil tightly around the contents to form a foil pack.

6. Bake at 180°C for 25–30 minutes or until cooked through.

Running straight home to surprise my wife with this meal ... It's going to be an amazing evening thanks to you, Foodies 😍😍😍😍😍

– ANNANIUS AZZARO

SAVOURY | 83

CHILLI CON CARNE SKILLET

A flavour-packed base of beans, mince and cheese, topped with fluffy garlic bread buns – this one is a winner!

1 tbsp olive oil
1 onion, chopped
2 cloves garlic, crushed
500 g beef mince
1 can kidney beans, drained
1 tbsp Robertsons cumin
1 tbsp Robertsons paprika
Knorr Naturally Tasty Chilli Con Carne sachet
1 can tomato and onion mix
1 cup grated cheddar cheese
¼ cup butter, melted
½ tsp Robertsons garlic salt
1 tbsp chopped parsley
1 kg raw prepared bread dough (found in supermarket fridges)
Flour for covering dough balls

1. In a medium ovenproof pan, heat the olive oil over medium heat. Add the onion and garlic and cook until translucent.

2. Add the mince and cook until browned. Once browned, stir in the kidney beans, cumin, paprika and the contents of the sachet.

3. Add the tomato and onion mix. Simmer for 5–10 minutes. Remove from the heat and sprinkle the grated cheese over the mince in the pan.

4. In a small bowl, combine the butter, garlic salt and parsley and whisk until combined.

5. Pull pieces off the dough and mould them into balls, rolling them in flour so that they are easier to work with.

6. Dunk each dough ball in the butter mixture and place it on top of the cooked chilli in the pan.

7. Bake in the pan at 180°C until the dough balls are golden and cooked through, about 45 minutes or until the bread topping is cooked and golden.

EPIC!!!
↓

CHILLI CON CARNE
STUFFED SWEET POTATOES

Packed with flavour and a whole bunch of your favourite ingredients, these might just be the tastiest stuffed sweet potatoes you will EVER eat!

4 sweet potatoes
Olive oil as indicated in recipe
Salt
500 g beef mince
2 red onions, chopped
1 red pepper, chopped
4 garlic cloves, crushed
2 tsp Robertsons paprika
2 tsp Robertsons cumin
1 tsp Robertsons origanum
1 tsp chilli powder
1 can tomato and onion mix
1 Knorr beef stock pot
Salt and pepper to taste
1 can kidney beans
1 cup grated mozzarella cheese
Smashed avocado
Sprouts

1. Poke holes in each sweet potato with a fork. Place the potatoes on a baking tray and drizzle with olive oil. Season with salt before baking at 180°C until soft.

2. Heat 1 tablespoon olive oil in a pot. Brown the mince and remove from the pan.

3. Heat 1 tablespoon olive oil in a large pot, fry the chopped onions, pepper and crushed garlic together with the paprika, cumin, origanum and chilli powder until fragrant.

4. Add the can of tomato and onion mix, beef stock pot, salt and pepper to taste and kidney beans to the pot. Stir to combine and add the cooked mince to the pot.

5. Slice open each sweet potato and stuff with the chilli con carne mixture.

6. Top with the grated cheese and bake in the oven at 180°C until the cheese is melted.

7. Serve with smashed avocado and sprouts.

Aweee, this is one deluxe and delicious recipe! Got my name on it!
– WILMA JANSE VAN RENSBURG

BREAD PIZZA

A super ch(easy) snack or light meal idea ...
Perfect for busy school nights and lazy weekends!

9 slices of white bread
Tomato paste
1 cup grated Parmalat cheddar cheese
½ cup salami rounds
½ cup button mushrooms, sliced
Salt and pepper to taste
1 tbsp oregano
1 avocado, sliced

1. Cut the crusts off the bread slices.

2. Arrange the slices of bread on a baking tray, making sure that they fit neatly into each other to make a 'pizza base'.

3. Spread tomato paste over the bread.

4. Sprinkle grated cheese onto the tomato base, making sure to cover the base completely.

5. Place salami rounds and mushroom slices on top of the cheese.

6. Season the base with salt, pepper and oregano.

7. Bake in the oven for 15 minutes at 180°C or until golden brown.

8. Serve with avocado slices.

SAVOURY | 87

SHEET PAN DINNER

One sheet pan ... and you're on your way to making a delicious and easy dinner for 2 – with very little washing up!

Handful Food Lover's Market green beans
1 Food Lover's Market red pepper
1 Food Lover's Market mielie, halved
Butter
Food Lover's Market extra virgin olive oil
6 Food Lover's Market potjie (baby) potatoes
4 Food Lover's Market pork rashers, or more depending on sheet size
Salt and pepper to taste
Food Lover's Market sweet BBQ sauce
Fresh thyme

FOR THE GRAVY
2 tbsp flour
1½ cups milk

1. Slice the ends off the green beans.
2. Remove the seeds and roughly chop the red peppers.
3. Top the mealie halves with a little butter and wrap in aluminium foil.
4. Coat the baking tray with a generous amount of extra virgin olive oil.
5. Stack the potjie potatoes into two pyramids in two corners of the tray.
6. Bake the potatoes for 20 minutes at 180°C.
7. Once baked, place the pork rashers onto the tray, drizzle the rashers with olive oil and season with salt and pepper. Place the foil-wrapped mielies on the tray and bake for 15 minutes at 180°C.
8. Place the green beans and red peppers on the tray. Baste the pork rashers with BBQ sauce and place a sprig of fresh thyme on each rasher. Season the ingredients with an extra drizzle of olive oil, salt and pepper before baking for an additional 10 minutes at 180°C.
9. Remove all the ingredients from the tray, add the flour and milk to the tray and cook over medium heat to make a gravy, stirring continuously until the gravy is smooth.
10. Serve all the ingredients with the gravy.

Soooo going to try this!!!! ❤️ 😍
– DINEO RANAKA

SO SIMPLE!

MASSIVE MINCE BUN BAKE

Fluffy buns + tasty mince + bubbling cheese = a simple, SUPER tasty way to feed a crowd!

- 8 tbsp butter
- 2 large onions, sliced
- 500 g beef mince
- Knorr Naturally Tasty Spaghetti Bolognese sachet
- Salt and black pepper to taste
- 1 tbsp olive oil
- 1 tbsp Robertsons garlic salt
- 1 tbsp Robertsons Italian herbs
- 12 hamburger buns
- 12 cheddar cheese slices
- 1 cup grated mozzarella cheese

1. Melt 2 tablespoons butter in a pan over medium heat. Add the onions and cook, stirring occasionally, until lightly caramelised.

2. In a large bowl, mix the mince with the contents of the sachet. Season with salt and pepper.

3. Heat the olive oil in a pan. Brown the mince in the oil and set aside once cooked.

4. In a separate pan, melt the remaining butter and season it with the garlic salt and Italian herbs.

5. Lightly grease a large baking sheet. Separate the tops from the bottoms of the hamburger buns. Fit the bottoms of the hamburger buns tightly on the baking sheet.

6. Place a slice of cheddar cheese on top of each bun.

7. Evenly distribute the mince and onion mixture on the bottom buns. Top with grated mozzarella cheese.

8. Close the buns and brush the butter mixture over the top buns.

9. Bake the hamburger buns at 180°C until the tops are lightly browned.

10. Serve immediately.

MAIZE BALLS IN A CREAMY BACON SAUCE

Mmmmm — this creamy maize bake will fast become one of the best-loved recipes in your home.

2 tbsp oil
1 onion, finely chopped
1 cup White Star super maize meal
1 tsp salt
1 tsp baking powder
1 egg
½ cup milk
3 tsp parsley
1 tsp paprika
1 pack diced bacon
½ cup chicken stock
1 can of tomatoes
1 cup cream
½ cup grated cheddar cheese

1. Preheat the oven to 180°C.

2. Grease a large baking dish.

3. Fry half the onion in a little oil until soft and set aside.

4. Combine the maize meal, salt and baking powder and mix well. Beat the egg and milk together and add to the dry ingredients.

5. Add the cooked onion, parsley and paprika, mixing well.

6. Shape the mixture into balls.

7. In a separate pan, fry the remaining onion and diced bacon until browned and crispy.

8. Add the chicken stock, tomatoes and cream to the pan and bring to the boil.

9. Simmer for 10 minutes before pouring the mixture over the mealie balls in the baking dish.

10. Bake for 20–25 minutes until the balls are cooked through.

11. Sprinkle grated cheese over the dish and grill for 5 minutes, until the cheese is golden and melted, and serve.

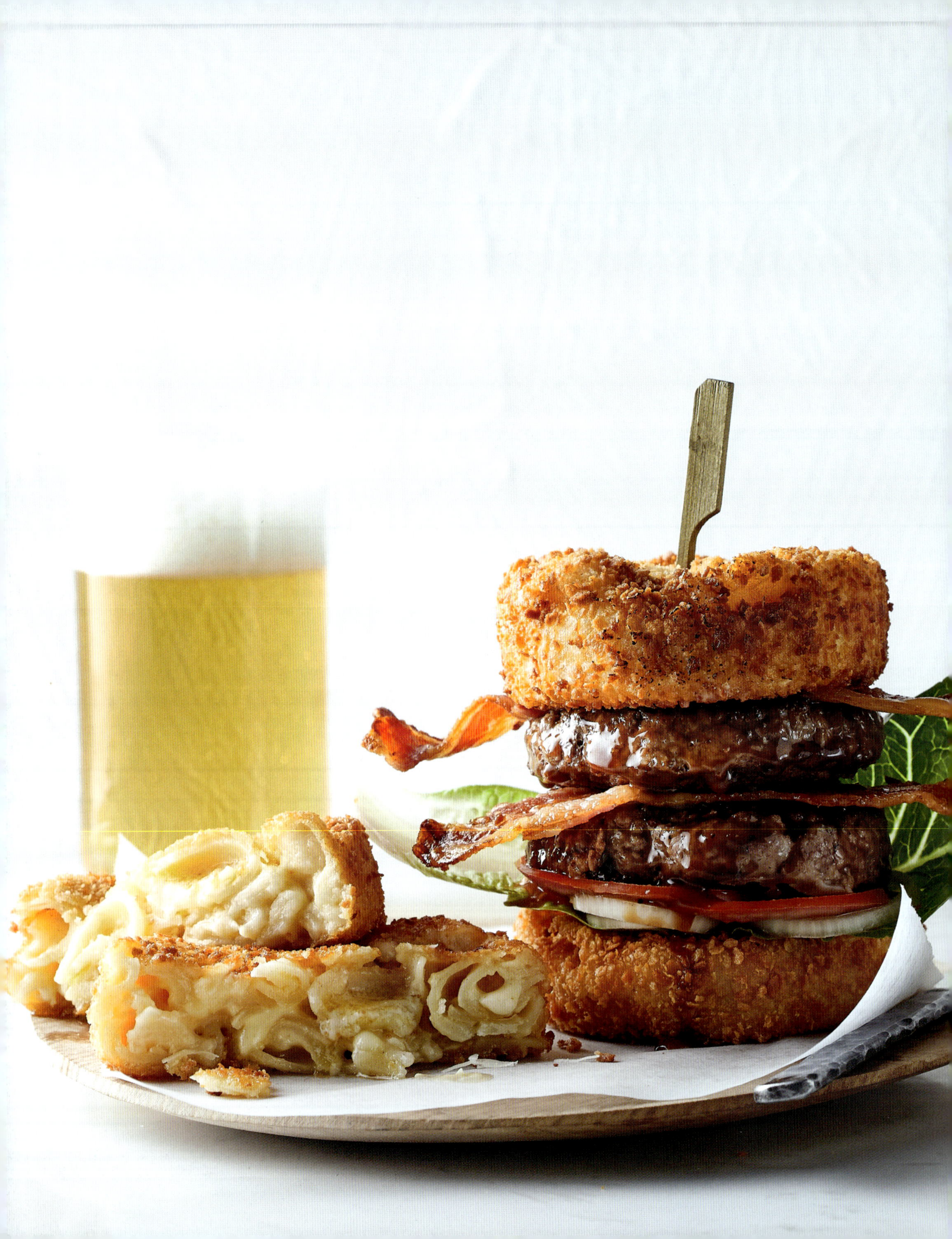

MAC 'N CHEESE BURGER

A deliciously cheesy macaroni 'bun' + a super meaty centre = the ultimate indulgence!

FOR THE MAC 'N CHEESE 'BUN'
500 g Fatti's & Moni's curved pasta shells
Pot of boiling water
1 tsp salt
3 tbsp butter
2 tbsp flour
2 cups milk
2 cups cream
4 cups grated cheddar cheese
Salt and pepper to taste
1 cup flour
3 eggs, whisked
2 cups breadcrumbs
Oil for deep frying

FOR SERVING
4 hamburger patties
4 slices of streaky bacon
Lettuce
Tomato
Onion

1. Boil the curved pasta shells in lightly salted water until cooked. Strain and set aside.

2. In a medium saucepan, melt the butter with flour. Once combined, pour in the milk and cream. Stir continuously and allow to thicken.

3. Add grated cheese to the mixture and stir to combine, season with salt and pepper.

4. Once the cheese has melted, pour in the drained pasta shells and combine.

5. Spread the mac 'n cheese over a baking tray lined with baking paper. Refrigerate until set.

6. Using a cookie cutter, cut the mac 'n cheese into circular shapes. Dip each circle into flour, egg and breadcrumbs before deep-frying in oil until golden and crispy.

7. Fry the hamburgers and bacon until cooked.

8. Assemble the burgers and serve.

SAVOURY | 93

BAKED SPAGHETTI PIE

Spaghetti bolognaise in PIE form – a creative and cost-effective recipe that the whole family will LOVE!

¾ pack spaghetti
1 tsp Robertsons Atlantic sea salt
1 tbsp olive oil
1 onion, chopped
3 cloves garlic, minced
500 g beef mince
2 tbsp tomato paste
1 can crushed tomatoes
1 Knorr beef stock pot
Salt to taste
2 tbsp Robertsons Italian herbs
3 eggs
1 cup grated cheese
Chopped basil leaves

1. Bring a pot of water to the boil, add the salt and the spaghetti. Once cooked, strain and set aside.

2. Heat the olive oil in a medium-sized saucepan, and brown the onion together with the garlic.

3. Once the onion is translucent, add the mince and cook until browned.

4. Add the tomato paste and crushed tomatoes to the pan and stir to combine.

5. Add the beef stock pot to the mixture and cook for 15 minutes.

6. Season with salt and Italian herbs.

7. Spoon out 2 cups of the mince and set aside.

8. Add the cooked spaghetti to the remaining mince and stir to combine. Add the eggs to the mixture.

9. Grease a cake tin with butter before adding the spaghetti mixture. Smooth the spaghetti with your spatula before covering with the 2 cups reserved mince and the grated cheese.

10. Bake at 180°C for 25 minutes.

11. Garnish with chopped basil leaves and serve.

> **My absolute favourite, will definitely try this.** 😍😍😍
>
> **– HLUB'ELIHLE THABISA MZAIDUME**

MMMMM...

SPAGHETTI TWO WAYS:

2X the flavour = 2X the fun ... pasta lovers, these two are for you!

SAUSAGE AND BEAN SPAGHETTI

½ pack Fatti's & Moni's spaghetti
Pot of salted boiling water
1 tsp salt
Olive oil for frying
1 onion, chopped
1 clove garlic, crushed
1 pack of Enterprise smoked Russians
1 can Koo four bean mix in brine
1 can All Gold Mediterranean-style peeled and diced tomatoes with aubergines and courgettes
1 cup baby spinach
Salt and pepper to taste
Fresh parsley, chopped
½ avocado, finely sliced
1 tomato, diced
Fresh parsley, chopped, as a topping

1. Add the spaghetti to a pot of salted boiling water. Boil for 5–8 minutes. Strain and set aside.
2. Heat olive oil in a medium saucepan. Fry the chopped onion and crushed garlic until fragrant.
3. Slice the smoked Russians and add to the pan.
4. Strain the beans and add to the pan, stirring to combine.
5. Add the Mediterranean-style tomatoes to the pan followed by the baby spinach. Stir and allow the spinach to wilt.
6. Simmer for a few minutes and season with salt and pepper.
7. Stir the cooked spaghetti through and add fresh parsley to the pan.
8. Mix together the sliced avocado and diced tomato for a relish.
9. Serve the spaghetti topped with a spoonful of the relish and fresh parsley.

> I tried two of your dishes already. Divine. Keep them coming!
> — MARLEY MAHLAKO HLAKUDI

CREAMY BACON ALFREDO

½ pack Fatti's & Moni's spaghetti
Pot of salted boiling water
1 tsp salt
Olive oil for frying
½ cups chopped onion
½ cups chopped mushrooms
1 pack Enterprise Bits-O-Bacon
3 tbsp butter
3 tbsp flour
2 cups cream
2 cups grated mozzarella

1. Add spaghetti to a pot of salted boiling water. Boil for 5–8 minutes. Strain and set aside.

2. Heat olive oil in a medium-sized saucepan. Add the chopped onion and mushrooms to the pan to brown.

3. Once browned, remove the onion and mushrooms from the pan and set aside.

4. Add the bacon to the pan and fry until crispy. Remove the bacon from the pan and set aside.

5. Melt the butter in the pan. Once melted, whisk in the flour. Add the cream to the pan, stirring continuously to avoid lumps.

6. Once thickened, add 1 ½ cups of the grated mozzarella and allow it to melt. Add the fried mushrooms, onions and most of the bacon (except for 2 tablespoons, for serving) to the Alfredo sauce and stir to combine.

7. Stir through the cooked spaghetti and pour the pan contents into a baking dish. Cover with the remaining ½ cup of cheese and bake for 10–15 minutes at 180°C until golden. Serve by sprinkling with the reserved bacon.

The chef I have become! Lately my family likes my cooking most days ...
– FUNEKA MAKITLA

SO CLEVER!

THREE-INGREDIENT PASTA IN A MUG

Three ingredients + a mug = the perfect hunger buster for busy weeknights or lazy weekends on the couch!

1 cup marinara sauce
2 cups grated mozzarella cheese
2 tsp fresh basil, chopped
½ pack Fatti's & Moni's pasta quills, cooked until al dente (firm to the bite)

1. Preheat the oven to 180°C.

2. Place a spoonful of the marinara sauce into the bottom of a wide-mouthed, oven-safe coffee mug.

3. Sprinkle 1–2 tablespoons of grated mozzarella on top, followed by some of the chopped basil and some more mozzarella cheese.

4. Generously cover the cheese with marinara sauce.

5. Working in a spiral motion, place the cooked pasta quills, tube-end facing up, in the cup on top of the marinara sauce.

6. Fill the mug snuggly with pasta so that the pasta will hold its shape after being baked.

7. Top the pasta with enough marinara sauce to cover it.

8. Sprinkle it with the remaining mozzarella cheese. Bake for 20 minutes.

9. Once the pasta is baked, place a plate on top of the mug, then flip it over to unmould the pasta onto the plate.

10. Garnish with chopped basil and serve.

SAVOURY | 99

JARS ON THE GO

A genius idea for on-the-go healthy meals ... pack them for lunches, picnics, camping and pretty much any other occasion!

1 cup Tastic brown rice
2 cups water
½ teaspoon salt
2 chicken breast fillets
Olive oil
Pinch of garlic salt
Pinch of pepper
Pinch of thyme
1 lemon, freshly squeezed
1 cup diced tomatoes
½ cup sweetcorn
1 wheel feta cheese, or more depending on preference
1 small avocado, sliced
2 small handfuls baby spinach leaves

FOR THE DRESSING
2 tbsp mustard
2 tbsp balsamic vinegar
4 tbsp olive oil
2 tbsp honey
Salt and pepper to taste

1. Bring the brown rice to the boil in lightly salted water. Simmer with the lid on for 25–30 minutes until the rice grains are plump and fluff apart with a fork.

2. Coat chicken breast fillets in olive oil, a pinch of garlic salt, pepper and thyme. Place the chicken breast fillets in a pan over medium heat, and add a dash of freshly squeezed lemon juice to the pan while frying.

3. Fry until cooked through, remove from the heat and shred the chicken.

4. Add some brown rice to the bottom of a mason jar, top the rice with shredded chicken, diced tomato, sweetcorn, feta, avocado slices and baby spinach. Use up all the ingredients until you have filled 4 jars or more depending on the size of your jars.

5. In a separate small jar, combine the dressing ingreidients. Shake until mixed.

6. Pour the dressing over the salad in the mason jar and enjoy on the go!

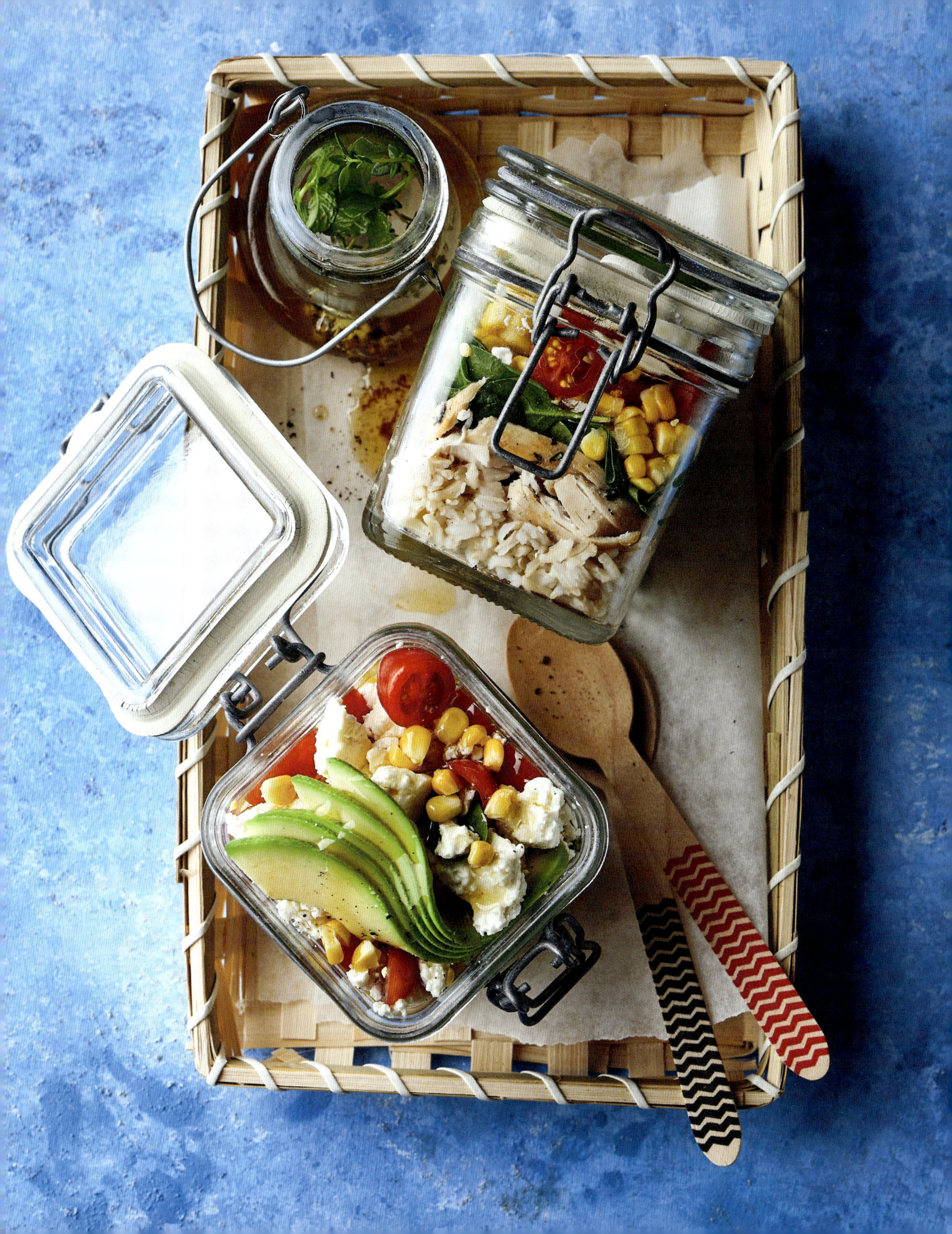

CHEESY RICE CASSEROLE

Bubbling cheese, tender chicken and fluffy rice ... Mmmmm!

1 cup Tastic parboiled rice
2 ½ cups water
½ tsp salt
2 chicken breast fillets
2 tbsp olive oil
1 tsp ground cumin
1 tsp garlic powder
½ tsp chilli powder
2 tbsp hot sauce (such as Tabasco)
400 g bottle chunky tomato salsa
1 cup sweetcorn
1 can black beans, rinsed or drained
1 ½ cups grated cheddar cheese

FOR THE GARNISH
Bunch chopped fresh coriander
1 cup sour cream
1–2 avocados

1. Bring the rice to the boil in lightly salted water.
2. Reduce the heat and allow to simmer for 20–25 minutes.
3. Preheat the oven to 180°C.
4. Butterfly the chicken breast fillets to allow for quicker cooking. Heat olive oil in a pan and cook the chicken, about 5 minutes each side.
5. Add the cumin, garlic powder and chilli powder 5 minutes from the end of cooking.
6. Remove from the heat and shred the chicken with two forks.
7. Add the cooked and drained rice to a large baking dish.
8. Add the chicken, hot sauce, salsa, sweetcorn and black beans to the dish and stir to combine thoroughly.
9. Sprinkle the cheese on top and bake uncovered for about 15 minutes, or until the cheese is melted.
10. Garnish with coriander, sour cream and avocado and serve.

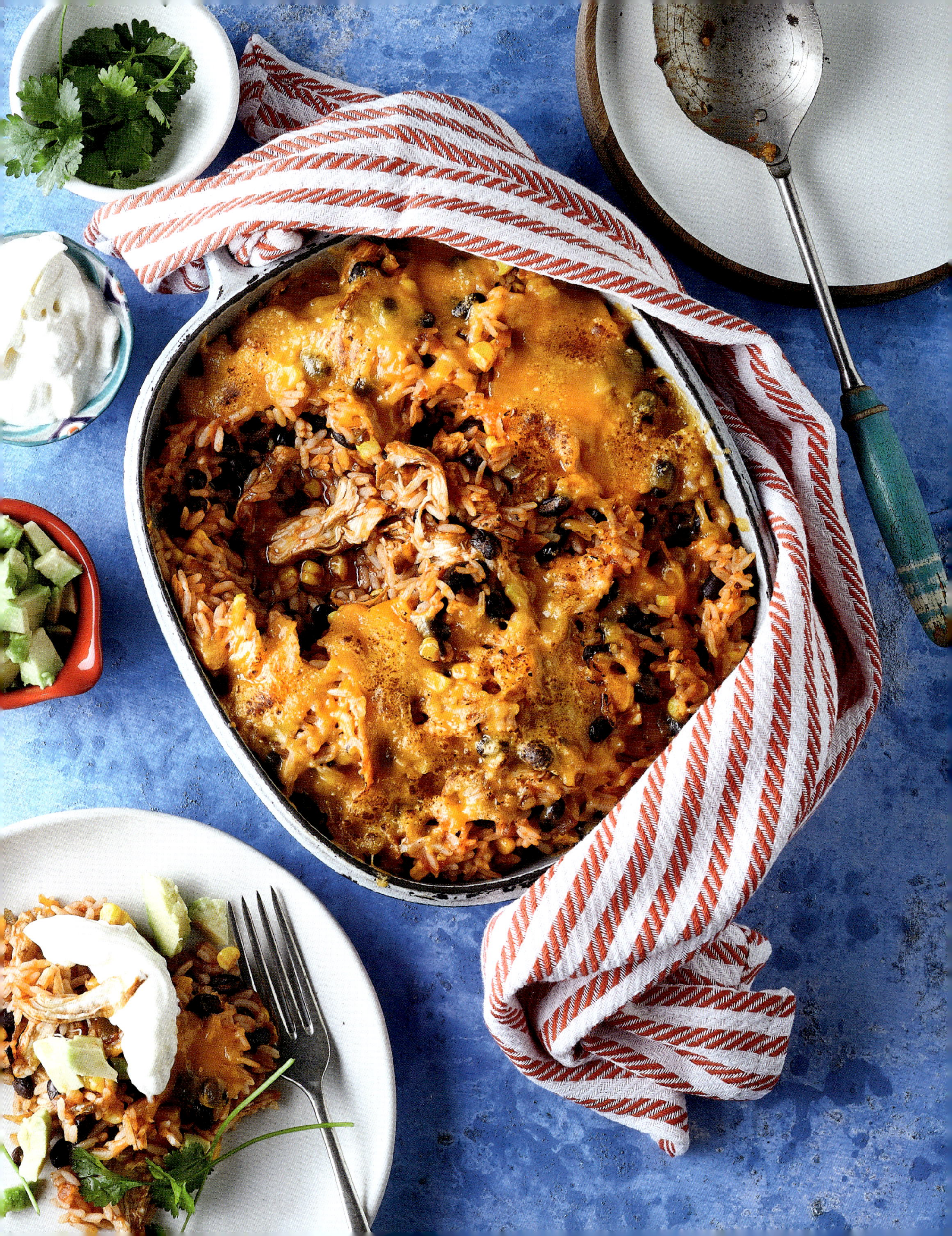

SUPER EASY FIVE-INGREDIENT RISOTTO

Silky smooth, fuss-free and packed with flavour! This five-ingredient risotto = 😃

2 chicken breasts, skin on but deboned (see the NOTE)
Salt and pepper to taste
Olive oil
2 cups mixed mushrooms, sliced
1 cup Tastic risotto rice
2 cups chicken stock
2 ½ cups Parmalat cream
Fresh basil, to garnish

NOTE: To debone the chicken breasts place the breasts, skin side up, on a clean cutting board. Using a boning knife, cut right next to the bone while pulling away the meat as you go. Use the bones for soup or for making stock.

1. Remove the skin from the deboned chicken breasts and set aside. Then cut the breasts into strips.
2. Season the chicken skin with salt and pepper and place under a hot grill until crisp.
3. In a large skillet, heat some olive oil over medium heat and fry the chicken until browned. Season with salt and pepper to taste. Remove from the pan and set aside.
4. Add the mixed mushrooms to the pan and cook until soft.
5. Add the risotto rice to the pan and stir to coat followed by the chicken stock, a little bit at a time, stirring throughout until it is completely absorbed.
6. Next, add 2 cups of the cream, slowly stirring throughout until it is absorbed.
7. Once absorbed, return the chicken to the pan.
8. Stir and heat through once more. Just before serving, add the last ½ cup of cream.
9. Season with salt and pepper and serve with the crisp pieces of skin.
10. Garnish with fresh basil and serve.

ONE-POT CHICKEN AND RICE

A no mess, no stress, DELICIOUS one-pot dinner ... Add all your ingredients to one pot, pop on the lid and voilà – tender chicken pieces on a bed of fluffy rice!

Olive oil
6 chicken thighs
Salt and pepper to taste
1 onion, chopped
2 garlic cloves, crushed
1 red pepper, chopped
¾ cup sun-dried tomatoes
1 cup Tastic parboiled rice
1 can crushed tomatoes
1⅓ cups chicken stock
Fresh basil leaves

1. Heat olive oil in a pan and braise the chicken thighs for 3–4 minutes until golden and crispy. Season with salt and pepper.

2. Remove the chicken from the pan and fry the chopped onion with the crushed garlic. Once browned, add the chopped red pepper, sun-dried tomatoes and rice.

3. Season with salt and pepper, add the crushed tomatoes and chicken stock. Return the chicken thighs to the pan and allow to cook for 40 minutes.

4. Garnish with fresh basil leaves and serve with veggies of your choice.

CABBAGE RICE ROLL-UPS

A ch(easy) and DELECTABLE rice dish you may never have dined on before!

½ cup Tastic brown and wild rice
2 cups boiling water
½ tsp salt
Olive oil
½ onion, chopped
1 cup mushrooms, chopped
1 cup baby spinach
1 tsp crushed garlic
½ can tomato and onion mix
12 whole cabbage leaves
1 jar (440g) marinara sauce
1 cup grated mozzarella

1. Bring the brown and wild rice to the boil in lightly salted water.

2. Reduce the heat and allow to simmer for 30–40 minutes until the rice kernels are tender. Drain any excess water and set aside.

3. Heat olive oil in a pan and brown the chopped onion with the chopped mushrooms, baby spinach and crushed garlic.

4. Once browned, add the rice to the mixture. Stir to combine.

5. Add the tomato and onion mix to the mixture and allow to simmer.

6. Using a knife, remove the centre of the cabbage so that you can easily remove the cabbage leaves.

7. Blanch the leaves in hot water.

8. Spoon the rice mixture into each leaf and roll up each leaf.

9. Place the roll-ups in a 30 × 20 cm casserole dish and baste them with marinara sauce and grated mozzarella cheese.

10. Bake at 180°C for 25 minutes.

11. Serve hot.

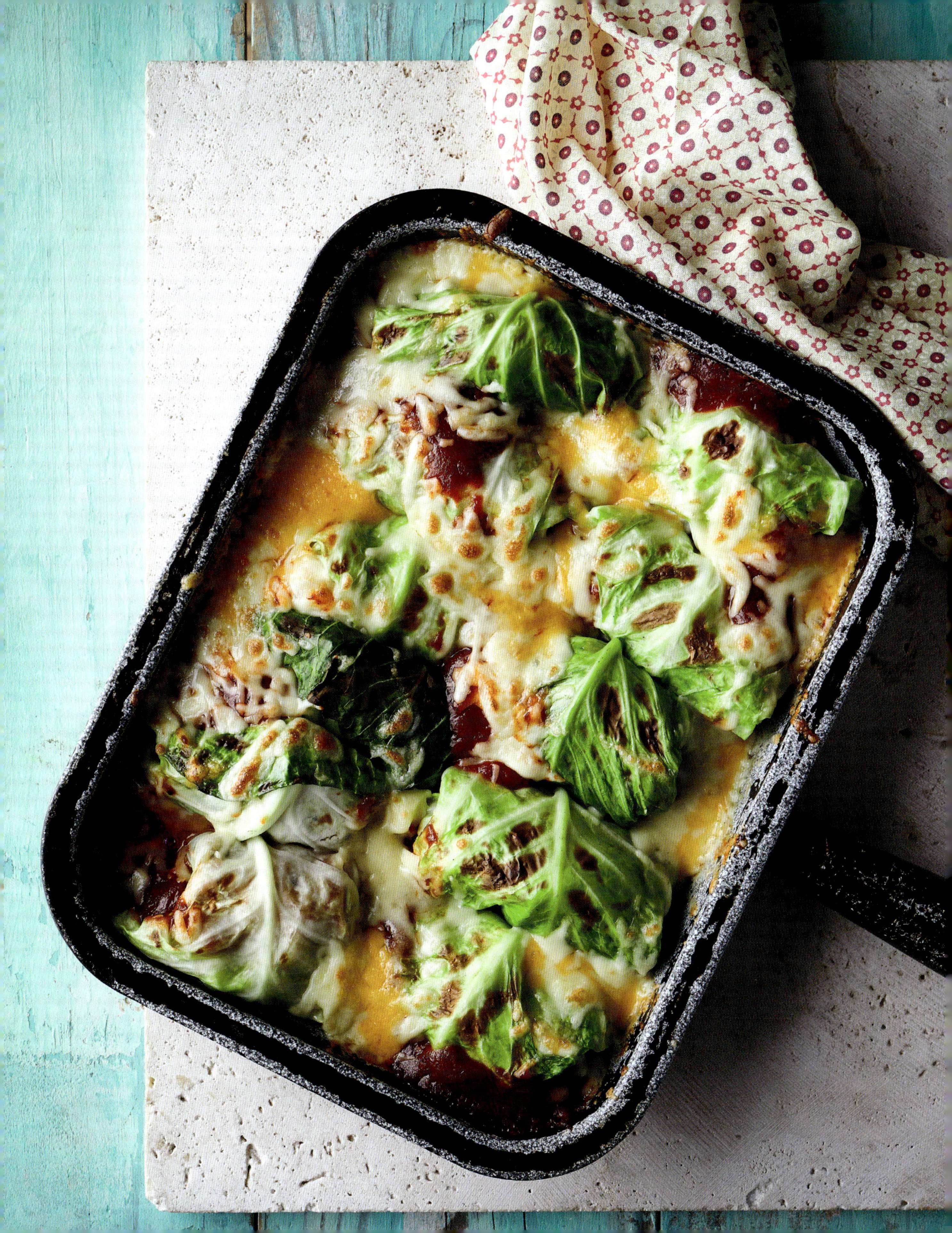

ME PLEASE!

RICE FRITTER STACK

A great way to use up leftovers and have some fun in the kitchen!

1 cup Tastic bonnet rice
3 cups boiling water
1 tsp salt
½ cup roughly chopped mushrooms
½ cup roughly chopped red and yellow peppers
1 cup cooked black beans
½ cup sweetcorn
1 cup grated zucchini (aka baby marrows or courgettes!)
⅓ cup breadcrumbs
⅖ cup cornflour
2 eggs
½ tbsp Worcestershire sauce
¼ tsp cumin
Salt and pepper to taste
1 tbsp olive oil

FOR SERVING
Avocado, smashed
Rosa tomatoes, halved
Crispy streaky bacon slices
Feta, crumbled
Creamy dressing

1. Bring the rice to the boil in lightly salted water and allow to simmer for 10–12 minutes. Drain any excess water and set aside.

2. In a food processor, blitz the roughly chopped mushrooms and set aside.

3. Repeat the process, individually blitzing the roughly chopped peppers, cooked black beans and sweetcorn.

4. Lastly, blitz the cooked rice.

5. Combine all the blitzed ingredients in a medium-sized mixing bowl with the grated zucchini, breadcrumbs, cornflour, eggs, Worcestershire sauce, cumin and salt and pepper to taste.

6. Using an ice cream scoop, scoop equal portions of the rice mixture onto square pieces of baking paper. Place a second piece of baking paper over the rice mixture and flatten, using a weight if needed.

7. Heat the olive oil in a pan before frying each rice fritter for 4–5 minutes until golden and crisp on each side.

8. Serve the fritters stacked with smashed avocado, halved rosa tomatoes, crispy bacon slices, crumbled feta and a creamy dressing.

UPSIDE-DOWN RICE BOWL

Too much month at the end of your money? Then this is for you!

1 cup Tastic brown rice
3 cups boiling water
½ tsp salt
1 green pepper, seeds removed
1 onion, peeled
1 tbsp olive oil for frying
1 tsp cumin
½ tsp garlic
1 tsp parsley
½ tsp paprika
Salt and pepper to taste
4 eggs
Chilli flakes (optional garnish)
Parsley (optional garnish)

1. Bring the brown rice to the boil in lightly salted water. Reduce the heat and allow to simmer for 30–40 minutes. Once cooked, drain any excess liquid.

2. Chop the green pepper and onion.

3. Heat the olive oil in a pan. Add the cumin, garlic, parsley and paprika and stir until fragrant. Add the green pepper and onion and cook until the onion is browned.

4. Season with salt and pepper.

5. Once any liquid has cooked away, add the rice to the pan, stirring to mix in the spices and green pepper and onion mixture.

6. Pack the rice tightly in 4 bowls, pat it down firmly, place a serving plate on top and flip, turning out so that you have a round shape.

7. In a separate frying pan, fry each egg sunny-side up.

8. Place the fried eggs on top of each rice dome.

9. Season with salt and pepper and sprinkle with chilli flakes and parsley before serving.

CHEESY BAKED FRITTER STACK

A meal that will warm your insides ... and a great option for a Meatless Monday!

FOR THE FRITTERS
1 cup White Star super maize meal
1 red onion, chopped
1 tsp ground cumin
1 tsp garlic powder
1 tsp baking powder
Salt and pepper to taste
1 egg
1 can sweetcorn, drained
2 tbsp milk
¼ tsp chilli powder
Sunflower oil

FOR STACKING
1 onion, chopped
1 cup mushrooms, chopped
Brie cheese, sliced
100 g (1 cup) grated cheddar cheese

FOR SERVING
Side salad ingredients of your choice

1. In a large mixing bowl, combine the maize meal, red onion, cumin, garlic powder, baking powder, salt, pepper, egg, sweetcorn (keep aside some sweetcorn for layering later), milk and chilli powder.

2. Heat oil for shallow-frying in a frying pan, and add spoonfuls of the mixture to the heated oil. The fritter sizes should range from large to small. Fry the fritters until golden and crispy.

3. In a separate pan, add a little oil and brown the onion and chopped mushrooms.

4. Stack the fritters from large to small, layering the reserved sweetcorn, the browned onions and mushrooms and Brie cheese slices between the fritters.

5. Top the stack with grated cheese before baking at 180°C for about 10 minutes or until the cheese is melted and crispy.

6. Serve with a side salad.

SAVOURY | 111

GREEN SPINACH
AND SPLIT PEA PIZZA

A light and healthy protein-packed pizza idea – health nuts, this one is for you!

½ cup Imbo split peas
1 cup water
4 cups baby spinach
½ tsp chia seeds
¼ cup almond flour
1 cup oat flour
¼ cup almond milk
½ tbsp apple cider vinegar
½ tbsp olive oil
½ tsp dried oregano
½ tsp dried basil
¾ tsp garlic powder
¾ tsp salt
Mozzarella cheese
Beetroot slices
Baby tomatoes, halved
Fresh herbs
Olive oil

1. Rinse the split peas under water until the water runs clear. Place the split peas in a saucepan with 1 cup water. Bring to the boil and simmer until soft.

2. In a separate pan, cook the baby spinach with a splash of water until wilted.

3. Once wilted, allow to cool and squeeze to release the excess water.

4. In a small bowl, mix the chia seeds with 1½ tbsp water. Put aside to set.

5. Blend the cooked and drained split peas together with the spinach until smooth.

6. In a mixing bowl, add the chia seeds, almond flour, oat flour, almond milk, apple cider vinegar, olive oil, oregano, basil, garlic powder and salt to the blended mixture.

7. Mix until smooth.

8. Spread the mixture onto a sheet of baking paper in a large oven pan and bake at 200°C for 20 minutes.

9. Add mozzarella pieces and bake for a further 10 minutes.

10. Top with beetroot slices, baby tomatoes, fresh herbs and olive oil before serving.

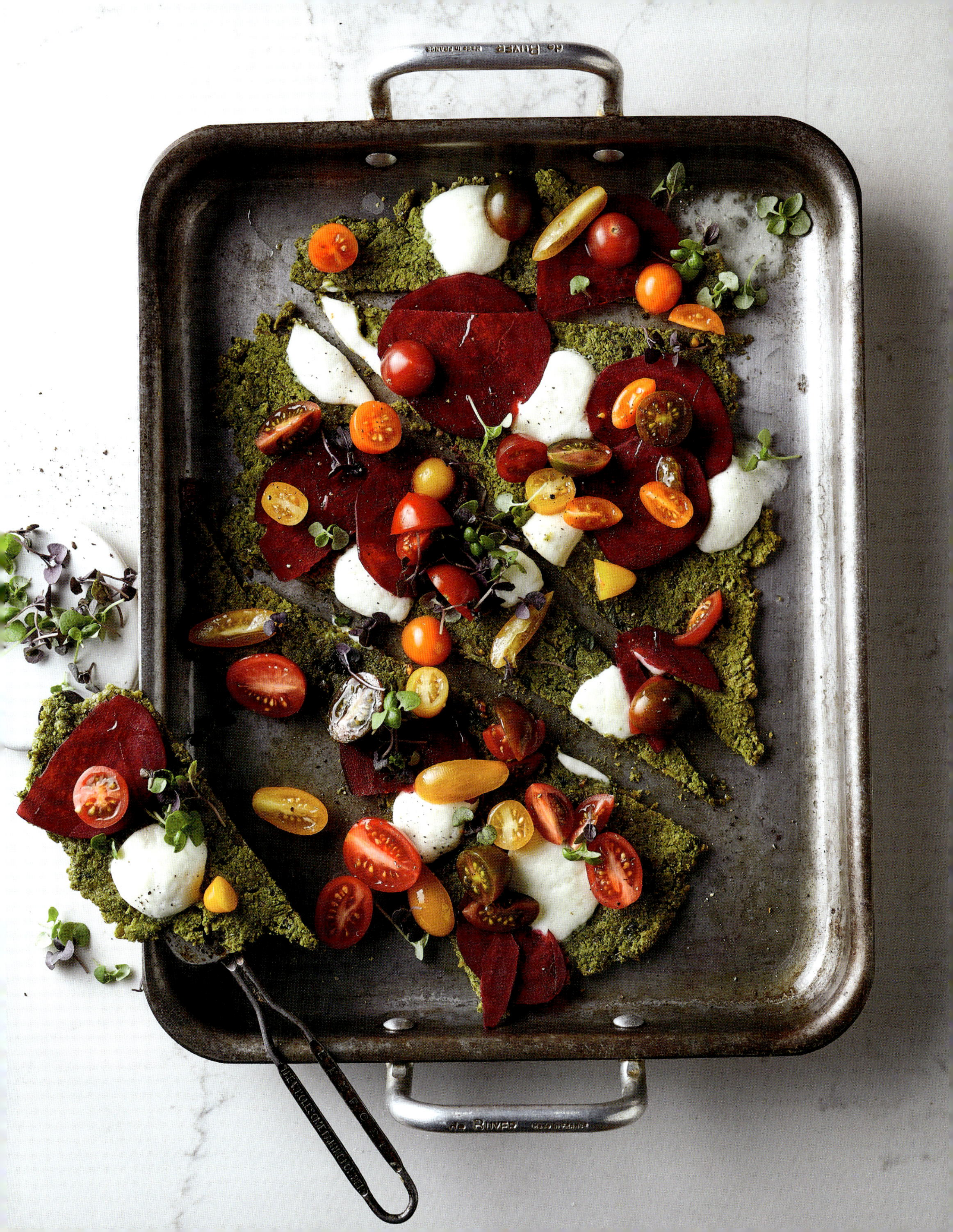

SHEET PAN FAJITA FEAST

Dinner prepped on a single sheet pan in just on 30 minutes!

2 tsp chilli flakes
1½ tsp ground cumin
1 tsp ground paprika
½ tsp ground coriander
Salt and freshly ground black pepper
1 red pepper
1 green pepper
1 yellow pepper
1 red onion
2 cloves garlic, crushed
3 tbsp olive oil
1 pack Fry's chicken-style strips
8 small flour tortillas
2 tbsp fresh lime juice
Fresh coriander, chopped
2 avocados, smashed
Vegan mayo
4 fresh limes for garnish

Yaaay!
Thanks for showing a vegan meal! ❤️
— ANKE BEHRENS

1. Preheat the oven to 180°C and spray a baking sheet with non-stick cooking spray.

2. In a small bowl, mix together the chilli flakes, cumin, paprika, coriander, 1½ teaspoons of salt and ½ a teaspoon pepper and set aside.

3. Remove the seeds of the peppers, cut them lengthways and slice the onion. Spread out the peppers on the baking sheet, leaving space to add the chicken-style strips later.

4. Sprinkle the sliced onion over the top of the peppers. Top with crushed garlic and the seasoning mix made in step 2, and drizzle with olive oil.

5. Roast the veggies in the preheated oven for 15 minutes.

6. Remove the baking sheet from the oven and add the chicken-style strips in the spaces and roast for another 10 minutes.

7. Once everything is cooked, mix the colourful layers together, and make a space in the corner to add the tortillas wrapped in aluminium foil.

8. Pop back into the oven for another 5 minutes for the tortillas to warm through.

9. Squeeze fresh lime juice over the sheet pan. Season with more salt to taste.

10. Assemble the wraps by topping with smashed avocados, a spoonful of vegan mayo, then fresh coriander, and garnish with slices of fresh lime.

VEGETABLE LASAGNE

Nourishing vegetables layered with creamy, cheesy goodness ... Mmmm!

1 tbsp olive oil
1 onion, finely chopped
2 garlic cloves, finely chopped
1 can tomato and onion mix
Knorr Naturally Tasty Lasagne sachet
Salt and pepper to taste
¼ cup butter
2 tbsp flour
2 cups milk
1½ cups grated mozzarella cheese
1 butternut, peeled and cut into 1cm-thick slices
2 cups baby spinach
Lasagne sheets
2 medium zucchinis, halved and sliced into noodles
½ cup grated cheddar cheese

> *That makes my mouth water with the promise of its delicious taste! Thanks for your healthy recipes! I'm gonna try them all!*
> **– MAGESH ZONDI MAMZONDI**

1. Heat the olive oil in a frying pan over medium heat. Add the onion and allow to soften. Then add the garlic, tomato and onion mix and the contents of the sachet.

2. Season with salt and pepper and simmer until sauce thickens.

3. Melt the butter in a saucepan over medium heat. Add the flour and stir to combine.

4. Gradually add the milk, stirring to prevent lumps forming until the sauce thickens.

5. Stir in 1 cup of the mozzarella and set aside.

6. Lightly grease a baking dish. Spoon half of the tomato mixture into the dish.

7. Arrange half the butternut over the tomato mixture followed by a layer of baby spinach. Place half of the lasagne sheets over the spinach, followed by the cheese sauce.

8. Repeat the layers a second time. For the topping, make a zucchini lattice. Layer zucchini noodles side by side at a diagonal in the baking dish. Lift the bottom half of every other noodle and lay another zucchini noodle across diagonally. Repeat until the top layer is full. Sprinkle the remaining mozzarella and the cheddar cheese over the lattice before baking.

9. Bake for 40 minutes at 180°C.

10. Serve hot.

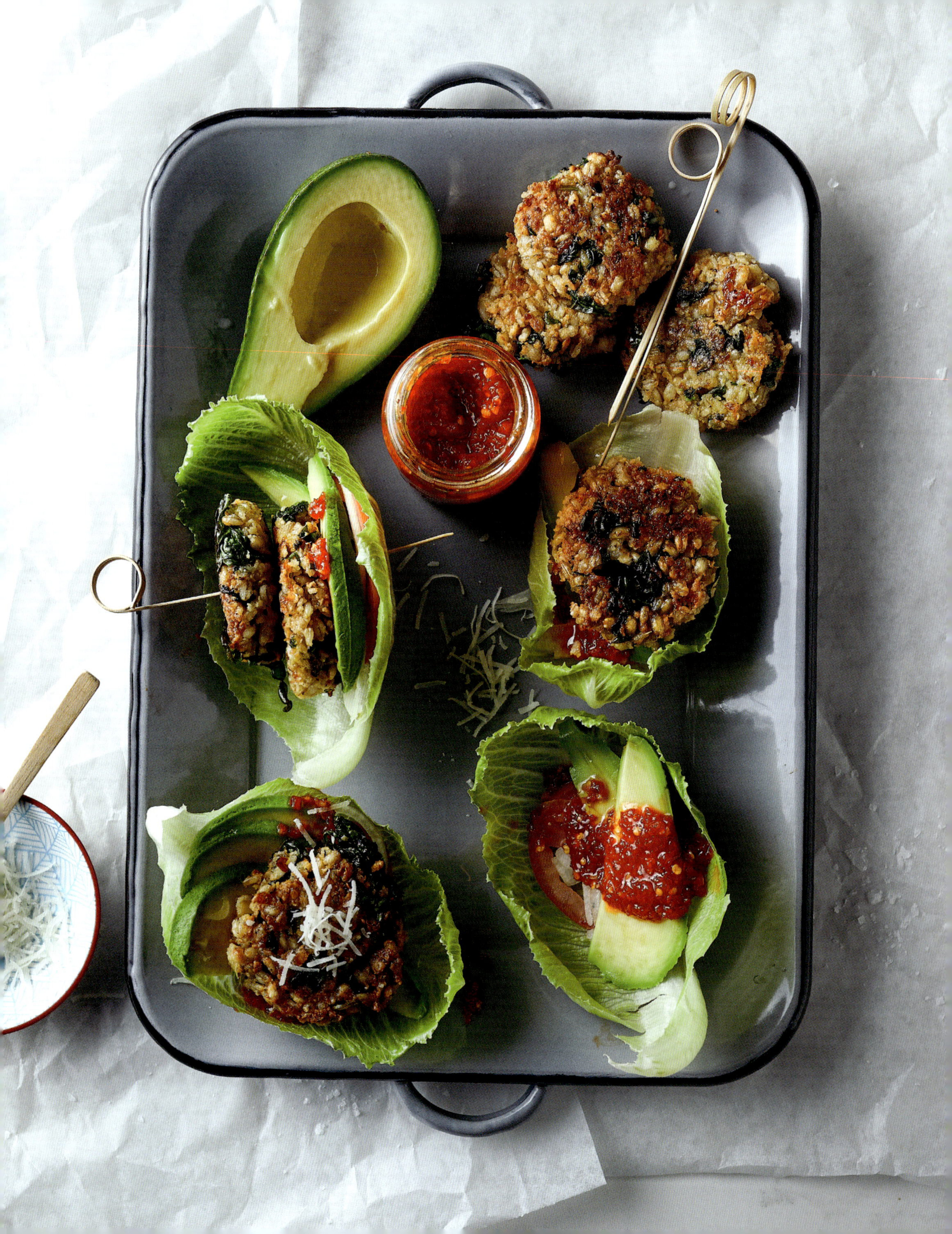

LETTUCE BURGERS

All of the fun, none of the bun ... These veggie-friendly BURGER BITES are super healthy, super tasty and easy to make. They're great as a light meal or a healthy snack when hosting friends and/or family!

⅓ cup Imbo barley
½ cup spinach
½ cup grated mozzarella cheese
½ cup breadcrumbs
1 tsp crushed ginger
3 garlic cloves, crushed
½ tsp red chilli flakes
½ tsp mixed dried herbs
Freshly ground black pepper to taste
Salt to taste
2 tsp cornflour
Oil for frying

TO SERVE
Lettuce leaves
Tomato slices
Onion rings
Avocado slices
Relish

1. Place barley in a large pot. Season with a pinch of salt. Add 2½ cups of water and cook on medium heat for about 25 minutes or until the barley is cooked. Allow to cool until at least lukewarm.

2. While the barley is cooking, wilt the spinach in a pan and drain off the excess water. Roughly chop the spinach and set aside.

3. In a large mixing bowl, add the cooked barley, cheese, breadcrumbs, ginger, garlic, red chilli flakes, mixed dried herbs and ground black pepper. Using a spoon, gently mix to combine everything.

4. Add the chopped spinach (ensure that all the water has been squeezed out) and mix again. Season with salt.

5. Add the cornflour and mix everything together gently.

6. Form a round flat burger pattie and set aside.

7. In a pan, heat the oil for frying.

8. When the oil is hot, reduce the heat to medium and place the burgers in the hot oil and fry on both sides until they are crispy and golden.

9. Serve the burger patties in a lettuce bun, topped with tomato, onion rings, avocado slices and your favourite relish.

SPICY LENTIL AND SPLIT PEA SOUP

A home-made, hearty soup idea that's loaded with cheese and flavour!

1 cup Imbo brown lentils
1 cup Imbo split peas
3 tbsp olive oil for frying
1 onion, chopped
2 stalks celery, chopped
1 carrot, chopped
2 cloves garlic, chopped
½ tsp turmeric
1 tsp paprika
½ tsp chilli powder
Salt and pepper to taste
8 cups vegetable stock
1 pack of bacon, diced
French loaf, sliced
Cheese, grated
Ground paprika for sprinkling

1. Rinse the lentils and split peas until the water runs clear.

2. In a large, ovenproof pot or casserole dish, heat the olive oil and add the chopped onion. Once browned, add the chopped celery, carrot and garlic. Once browned, add turmeric, paprika, chilli powder, and salt and pepper.

3. Stir to coat the vegetables before adding the drained lentils, split peas and vegetable stock.

4. Bring to the boil and reduce to a simmer for 60 minutes.

5. Spread diced bacon evenly on a tray. Grill until crispy. Drain any excess oil and set aside.

6. Using a hand-held blender, blend the soup until smooth. Divide the soup into individual ovenproof serving bowls.

7. Top slices of French loaf with grated cheese and place on top of each bowl of soup. Place the bowls into the oven (either on grill or at 180°C) and allow the cheese to melt.

8. Once ready, serve the soup with the crispy diced bacon pieces and a sprinkling of paprika.

PASTA PIE

If there's one recipe to try this winter, let it be this cheesy, meaty pasta pie!
Your family and friends will love you for it!

500 g Fatti's & Moni's Pasta Quills
Pot of boiling water
1 tsp salt
500 g beef mince
Olive oil
Salt and pepper to taste
2 cups marinara sauce
1 cup grated parmesan cheese
1 cup grated mozzarella cheese
1 cup grated cheddar cheese
Fresh basil

Would love a birthday cake like this ...
– KOOS ROESTOFF

1. Boil the pasta quills in lightly salted water until slightly underdone.

2. Drain and set aside.

3. In a separate pan, brown the beef mince in olive oil, seasoned with salt and pepper.

4. Once browned, add the marinara sauce and allow to simmer.

5. Add 1 cup grated parmesan and ½ cup grated mozzarella cheese to the drained pasta quills and mix to coat the pasta.

6. Place the pasta quills vertically into a cake tin so that they are tightly compacted together with no gaps.

7. Spoon the mince over the vertical pasta quills, pressing the mince into the quills.

8. Bake at 200°C for 20 minutes.

9. Remove from the oven and cover with the remaining ½ cup mozzarella cheese and the cheddar cheese.

10. Grill for 5 minutes at 200°C until the cheese is bubbling and crispy.

11. Garnish with fresh basil, slice and serve.

SAVOURY | 119

LENTIL AND SPLIT PEA
SHEPHERD'S PIE

A tasty mixture of lentils and split peas, topped with a silky layer of sweet potato, this dish has 'cozy home food' written all over it ... without compromising health goals!

3–4 sweet potatoes, washed
Salt and pepper
Fresh thyme
Olive oil
1 cup Imbo lentils
1 cup Imbo split peas
3 tbsp milk
1 carrot, diced
2 stalks of celery, diced
1 onion, diced
1 can chopped tomatoes
Handful chopped basil
1 cup chopped spinach
2 tbsp soya sauce
1 cup vegetable stock
Fresh basil, to serve

1. Using a potato peeler, peel the sweet potatoes. Place the potato skins on a lined baking tray and season with salt, pepper and fresh thyme and drizzle with olive oil. Toss to coat the skins and bake at 180°C for 15 minutes. Drain on paper towels and set aside.

2. Slice the sweet potatoes and boil in water for 15–20 minutes.

3. Rinse the lentils and split peas together in a colander until the water runs clear. Once rinsed, simmer for 30 minutes in boiling water. Drain and set aside.

4. Mash the cooked sweet potatoes with 1 tablespoon of the milk and salt until smooth.

5. In a large pan, soften the diced carrot, celery and onion with 2 tablespoons of water. Add the cooked lentils and split peas and mix to combine.

6. Add the chopped tomatoes together with the chopped basil, spinach and soya sauce. Stir in the vegetable stock.

7. Simmer for 10–15 minutes.

8. Place the mixture into small casserole dishes, topped with an even layer of sweet potato.

9. Bake at 180°C for 20 minutes.

10. Serve with fresh basil and crunchy potato skins.

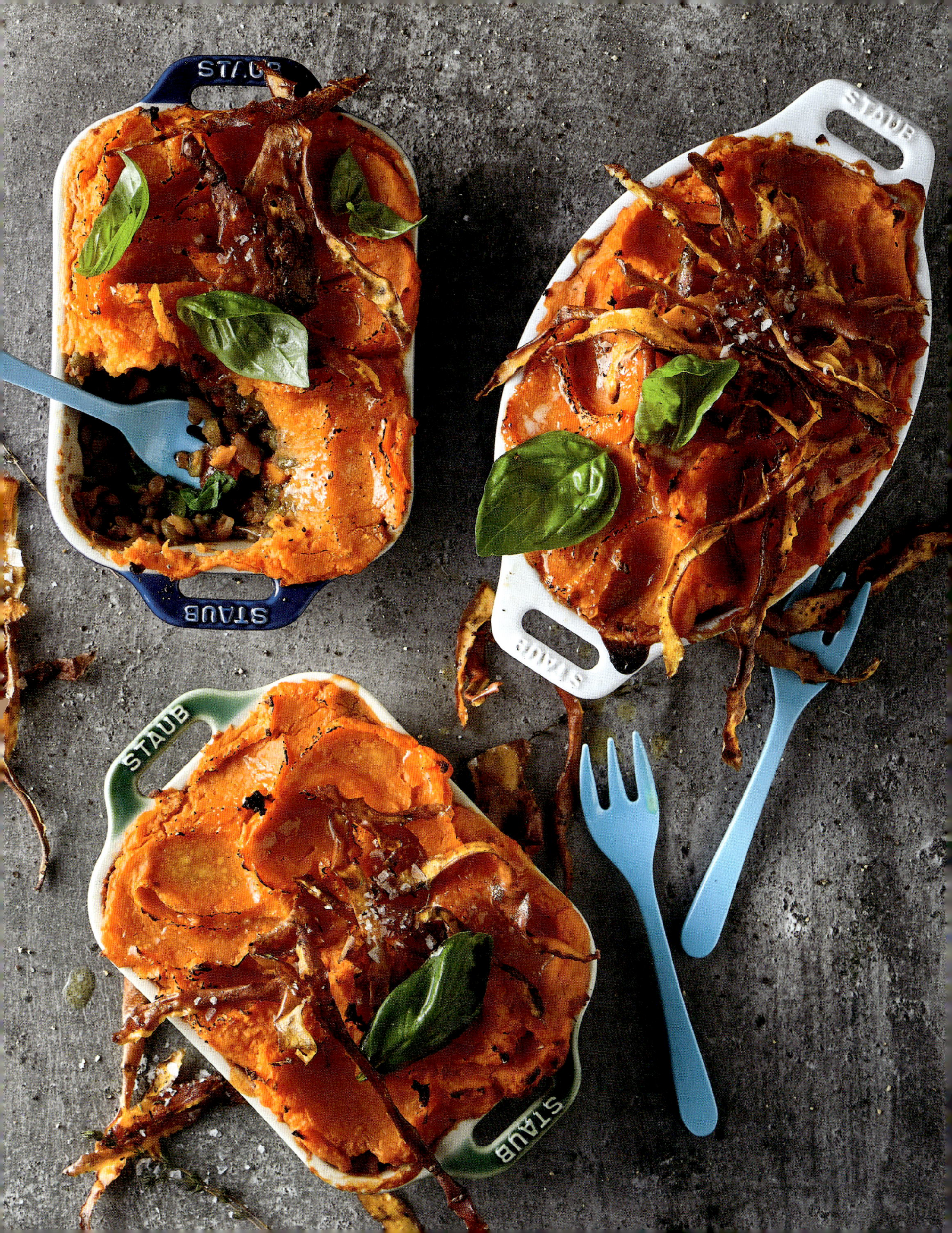
STAUB
STAUB
STAUB
STAUB
STAUB

STUFFED SWEET POTATOES

Quick, easy and delicious, you can whip up these
in a flash … All without breaking the bank!

4 sweet potatoes
1 cup Imbo brown lentils
2 cups water
1½ cups crumbled feta
Olive oil to drizzle
1 avocado
Salt and pepper to taste
Juice of 1 lime
1 tbsp chilli flakes
Sprouts (optional)
Pumpkin seeds (optional)
2 tbsp fresh coriander, chopped

1. Preheat the oven to 180°C.

2. Poke holes in the sweet potatoes with a fork and bake at 180°C for 45–60 minutes.

3. Add the brown lentils to 2 cups water, simmer for 30 minutes.

4. Strain and allow to cool.

5. Slice the baked sweet potatoes in half.

6. Scoop out the sweet potato centre.

7. Mix the sweet potato centre with the cooked lentils and fill the sweet potato halves with the mixture.

8. Sprinkle with feta and drizzle with olive oil before baking for 10 minutes at 180°C.

9. In a separate bowl, mix the avocado with salt, pepper and lime juice until smooth.

10. To serve, top the sweet potatoes with avocado mixture, chilli flakes, sprouts and pumpkin seeds if using, and fresh coriander for the garnish.

BEAN BURGERS

Beans are a great way to save money AND reduce your meat intake – health nuts, veggie heads and eco-warriors, this one is for you!

± 1 cup Imbo kidney beans
± 1 cup Imbo small white beans
3 cups cold water
1 cup grated zucchini
¼ cup spring onion
2 tbsp fresh coriander
1 tbsp cumin
1 tsp paprika
Lemon zest
1 tsp crushed garlic
¼ cup breadcrumbs
Salt and pepper to taste
1 egg
Flour for coating
Olive oil for frying
Seeded hamburger rolls
Lettuce
Cheese slices or grated cheese
Avocado (optional)
Shredded cabbage (optional)
Sweet chilli sauce (optional)

1. Pour the kidney beans and small white beans into a bowl, add water to cover and soak overnight.

2. Drain the beans and cook in 3 cups cold water, bring to the boil and cook until soft. Drain the beans once cooked.

3. Place the beans in a large mixing bowl and mash them.

4. Add the grated zucchini, spring onion, fresh coriander, cumin, paprika, lemon zest, breadcrumbs, salt, pepper and egg to the mashed beans.

5. Stir the mixture until combined.

6. Form patties with the mixture and coat with a dusting of flour.

7. Heat olive oil in a pan and fry the patties until golden brown and crispy.

8. Assemble each seeded hamburger roll with a patty, lettuce, cheese, avocado, shredded cabbage and sweet chilli sauce if using.

ROAST BUTTERNUT SALAD

Three easy, wholesome and yummy recipes featuring an all-time favourite vegetable ... you BUTTERNUT miss this one!

1 butternut, diced
Baby onions, halved
Food Lover's Market extra virgin olive oil
1 cup Food Lover's Market walnuts
¼ cup sugar
1 tbsp butter
Baby spinach, washed
Cooked beetroot, cubed
Avocado slices
Feta cheese, roughly crumbled
Food Lover's Market balsamic vinegar

1. Place the diced butternut and baby onions on a roasting tray, top with a drizzle of olive oil and bake for 25 minutes at 180°C.

2. In a saucepan, fry the walnuts with sugar and butter for 5 minutes until caramelised.

3. Place the washed baby spinach into a salad bowl, topped with the roasted butternut and onion, beetroot, avocado slices, crumbled feta and candied walnuts.

4. Top with a drizzle of olive and a drizzle of balsamic vinegar before serving.

Yummy! ♥ I love the veggie recipes.
— JAUNITA NAIDOO

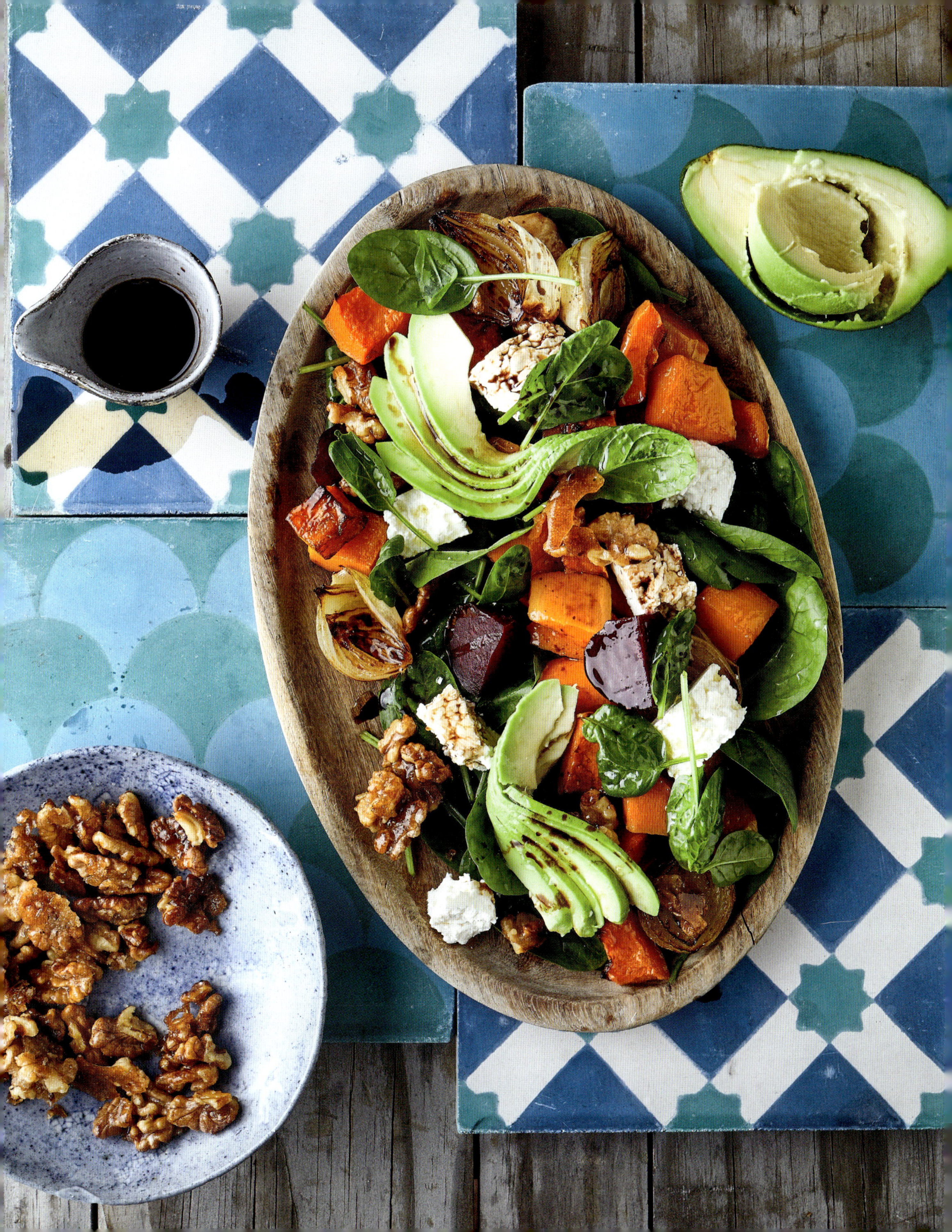

BUTTERNUT SOUP

1 butternut, peeled and chopped
1 onion, diced
1 red bell pepper, chopped
2 tbsp Food Lover's extra virgin olive oil
Salt
Pepper
Garlic paste
4 slices Food Lover's Market streaky bacon
Fresh thyme
1½ cups chicken stock
1½ cups Food Lover's Market coconut milk
Cream, to serve
Chives, chopped

1. On a large roasting tray, spread out the butternut, onion and pepper, evenly coated with olive oil.

2. Season with salt, pepper and garlic paste before baking for 25–30 minutes at 180°C.

3. In a frying pan, cook the bacon until crispy. Remove from the pan, crumble or dice into bits and set aside.

4. Place the roasted vegetables into a large pot and season with salt, pepper and fresh thyme.

5. Add the chicken stock and coconut milk.

6. Simmer for 5–10 minutes.

7. Blend with a hand-held blender until smooth.

8. Serve with a dollop of cream, chopped chives and crispy bacon bits.

STUFFED BUTTERNUT

1 butternut
Food Lover's Market extra virgin olive oil
1 onion, diced
½ red pepper, diced
½ green pepper, diced
2 tbsp tomato paste
2 cups vegetable stock
½ cup couscous
Salt and pepper
1–2 cups grated Food Lover's Market white cheddar cheese
Fresh parsley, to serve

1. Cut the butternut in half lengthways. Use a spoon to remove the seeds.

2. Coat the butternut halves in olive oil and bake for 1 hour at 180°C.

3. Meanwhile, in a frying pan, brown the diced onion with the diced red and green peppers. Add the tomato paste and stir until mixed before adding the vegetable stock.

4. Bring to the boil, remove from the heat and add the couscous.

5. After 5 minutes, fluff the couscous with a fork.

6. Season with salt and pepper.

7. Add a handful of the grated cheese to each butternut half, topped with a tablespoon of the couscous mixture.

8. Sprinkle more cheese on top and bake at 180°C for 5–10 minutes.

9. Serve with fresh parsley.

SAVOURY

STUFFED PEPPERS

Filling, cheesy and mouth-watering – a go-to weeknight dinner idea for the colder months!

1 cup Tastic jasmine rice
3–4 cups water
1 tsp salt
1 onion, chopped
1 clove garlic, crushed
1 tbsp olive oil
½ cup sweetcorn
½ cup kidney beans
2 tbsp fresh coriander, chopped
1 cup tomato, finely diced
¼ tsp chilli powder
1 tsp smoked paprika
Salt and pepper to taste
4 bell peppers
Grated cheddar cheese

1. Soak the jasmine rice for 15 minutes.
2. Bring the rice to a boil in lightly salted water. Cook for 15 minutes.
3. Drain and set aside.
4. Brown the chopped onion and crushed garlic in the olive oil.
5. Once browned, add the sweetcorn, kidney beans, chopped fresh coriander, finely diced tomato, chilli powder and smoked paprika to the pan and stir to combine.
6. Add the mixture to the cooked rice and season with salt and pepper.
7. Hollow out the peppers, making sure to remove all the seeds.
8. Spoon the rice mixture into each pepper and top with grated cheese.
9. Bake at 180°C for 20–25 minutes and serve.

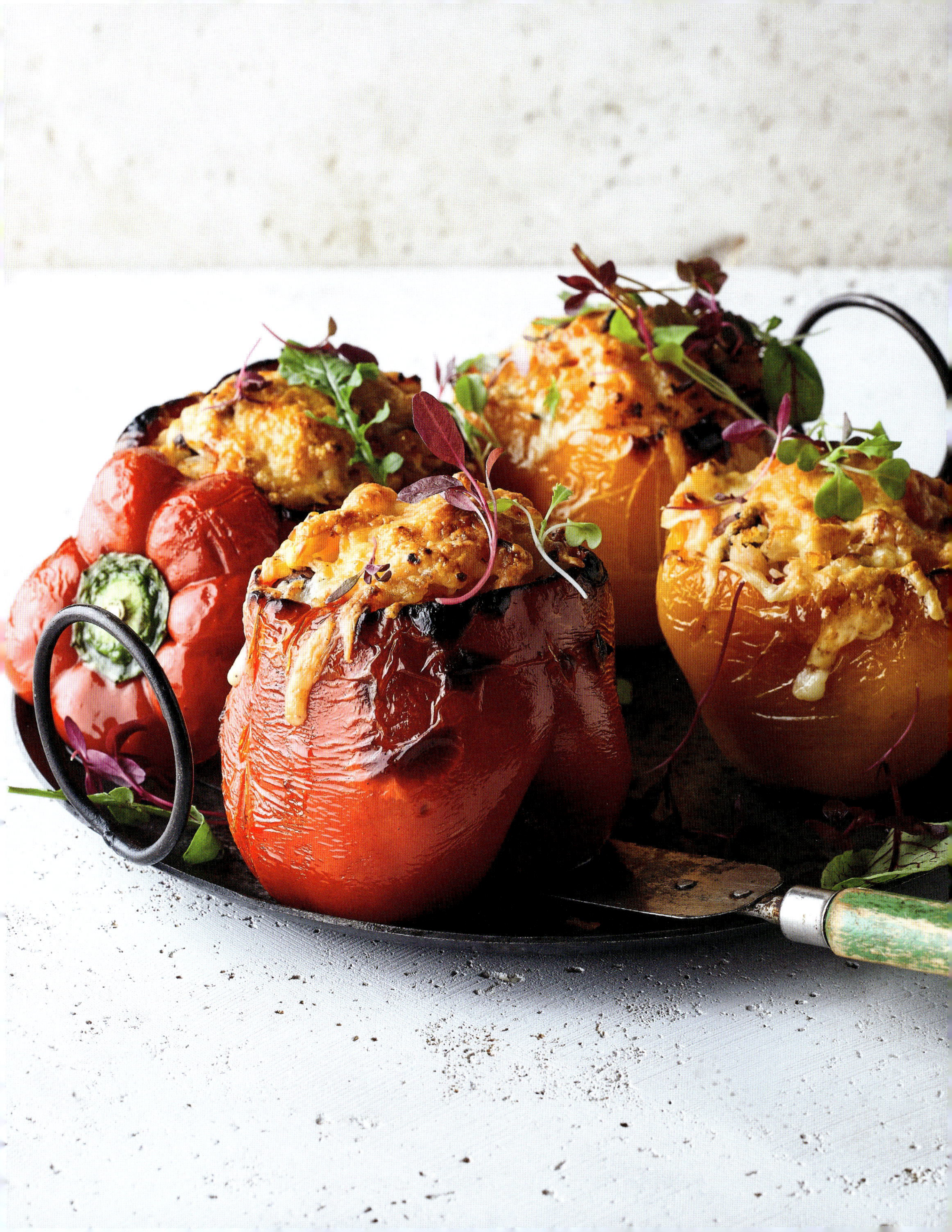

SIZZLING!

ON THE BRAAI

RIBEYE ON A CEDAR PLANK WITH A BONE MARROW CROSS-SECTION

A thick and juicy ribeye steak cooked on a charred cedar plank for a smoky flavour. Top with bubbling marrow and serve with a side of delicious crispy chips and a cold one!

1 garlic clove
⅓ cup olive oil
2 marrow bones
Robertsons rustic garlic and herb
2 x 350 g ribeye steaks
Robertsons traditional braai mix

SPECIAL REQUIREMENTS
1 Weber kettle braai
1 Weber cedar plank

1. Soak the cedar plank in water for 1 hour.

2. Finely chop garlic and add to a small bowl with olive oil, stir to combine.

3. Baste the marrow bones with the olive oil mixture. Season with the garlic and herb seasoning.

4. Season the ribeye steaks with the braai mix.

5. Fill one half of the Weber with charcoal and light a fire. NOTE: It is important that one half of the Weber has direct heat and the other has indirect heat.

6. Place the cedar plank onto the grid over the coals in the Weber and char for 3 minutes until blackened. Flip the cedar plank over onto the indirect side of the Weber (blackened side up).

7. Place the ribeye steaks onto the grid over the coals and sear for 2–3 minutes. Flip the steaks (browned side up) onto the cedar plank.

8. Place the marrow bones on the indirect heat side of the Weber.

9. Close the Weber's lid and make sure the holes are open. Allow to cook for 25 minutes.

10. Remove the ribeye steaks from the Weber and allow to rest for around 10 minutes. If the marrow has not started bubbling yet, leave it in the Weber, lid closed, holes open, while the ribeye rests.

11. Scoop the marrow onto the ribeye steaks and serve.

BOERIE PIES

Pieces of boerie cooked to your liking, encased in a flaky pie crust = a SUPER tasty braai idea!

3 onions
2 tbsp olive or sunflower oil
3 portobello mushrooms
300 g boerewors of choice
　(NOTE: do not use coiled boerewors)
Flour for dusting
1 roll Today puff pastry, thawed
Cheddar cheese
1 egg
1 tbsp water

SPECIAL REQUIREMENTS
1 Weber kettle braai

1. Pack one half of the Weber with coals and leave the other half open. Light the coals.

2. Peel, dice and fry the onions in the oil.

3. Dice and sauté the mushrooms in another pan (or remove the onions and set aside before cooking the mushrooms).

4. Once the coals are ready, braai your boerewors to your preference. Once cooked, remove the boerewors from the grid and close the Weber with the lid. Let the boerewors cool.

5. Sprinkle a kitchen surface with some flour to stop the pastry from sticking. Roll out the pastry and cut it into 4 rectangles.

6. Lay a strip of the fried onions down the middle of one of the pastry rectangles.

7. Lay a strip of the sautéed mushrooms on top of the fried onions.

8. Cut a piece of the cooled boerewors and place it on top of the mushrooms.

9. Grate some cheddar cheese over the boerewors.

10. Carefully fold the sides of the pastry over the boerewors, close and seal it so that it doesn't come apart when baking.

11. Cut thin, horizontal strips down the length of the pastry.

12. Brush the pastry with egg wash, made by mixing the egg and the water.

13. Prepare the other three rectangles of pastry in the same way.

14. Place the boerie pies in a foil container and place in the Weber, on the side without coals.

15. Close the lid and allow to bake for 30–35 minutes.

16. Allow the boerie pies to cool for 5–10 minutes before serving.

VEGGIE NICE BRAAI PIES

Yip, meat-free braais are totally possible ... here's proof!

Olive oil for frying
1 white onion, sliced
Fresh thyme
Salt and pepper to taste
1 punnet button mushrooms, wiped and sliced
2 cloves garlic, crushed
1 box Fry's mince with vegan gravy
1 small can tomato paste
2 rolls puff pastry, defrosted
Olive oil for brushing

TO SERVE
Braaied mielies
Fresh lettuce
Baby tomatoes
Carrot slivers
Cucumber
Red pepper
Chutney
Vegan mayo
Micro herbs for garnishing

Foodies of SA, you have outdone yourselves with this recipe! We are having dreams about this Braai Pie!
— FRY'S FAMILY

1. Heat the oil in a pan and gently fry the onion until soft. Add some fresh thyme and season with salt and pepper. Once the onions have caramelised, remove from heat and set aside.

2. Fry the sliced mushrooms and crushed garlic in a little oil until the mushrooms begin to soften and brown. Set aside.

3. In a separate pan, prepare the Fry's mince with vegan gravy according to the instructions on the pack. Add the tomato paste and cook for another 5 minutes before setting aside. The mince shouldn't be too wet.

4. Spray the braai grid with baking spray on both sides.

5. Unroll one of the rolls of puff pastry onto the grid.

6. Spoon the mince onto the puff pastry and spread it out to create an even layer, leaving a 2cm border around the edges of the pastry.

7. Top with a layer of mushrooms and a layer of onions. Break a few thyme leaves over the ingredients and season with salt and pepper.

8. Unroll the second layer of puff pastry over the top and fold the edges of pastry over and press gently to seal well.

9. Brush the top of the pie with olive oil.

10. Close the grid and braai the pie over medium coals, turning the grid regularly, for 15 minutes or until the pastry is crispy and cooked through.

11. Cut into squares and serve with braaied mielies and a fresh summer salad with a chutney/vegan mayo dipping sauce.

12. Garnish with fresh micro herbs and serve.

PAP IN A PUMPKIN

Impress your guests with this creative accompaniment to your next braai!

2 cups water
2 cups White Star super maize meal
1 red onion
1 green pepper
2 cloves garlic
1 thumb-sized piece of ginger
1 pumpkin
Salt and pepper to taste
2 cinnamon sticks
45 ml olive oil
1 can chopped tomatoes
½ cup chicken stock
1 tsp paprika
1 can baked beans in tomato sauce
200 g bacon bits
1 cup grated mozzarella cheese

SPECIAL REQUIREMENTS
Weber griddle pan

NOTE: This recipe can be done either in a Weber kettle braai or in the oven. The same cooking times apply to both.

1. Add the water to a pot and bring to the boil. Add the maize meal to the boiling water. Cook over moderate heat for 15–20 minutes. Fluff the porridge with a fork once cooked.

2. Finely chop the red onion, green pepper, garlic and ginger. Set aside.

3. Prepare a fire in the Weber with two-sided indirect heat.

4. Prepare the pumpkin by cutting a circle on top to make a lid. Remove the lid and clean the inside of the pumpkin using a spoon.

5. Place the pumpkin on the Weber griddle pan and add salt, pepper and cinnamon sticks.

6. Replace the lid and place the pumpkin on the Weber griddle pan, in the middle of the grid in the Weber and leave for 10 minutes.

7. Add the olive oil to a pan and sauté the chopped onion, green peppers, garlic and ginger over a medium heat.

8. Add the can of chopped tomatoes, chicken stock and paprika, and salt and pepper to taste to the pan.

9. Stir to combine before adding the baked beans and cook for a further 5 minutes.

10. Mix ½ of the tomato mixture with the cooked pap. Set aside the remaining tomato mixture.

11. In a separate pan, fry the bacon bits until golden and crispy.

12. Remove the pumpkin from the Weber and stuff the pumpkin with the maize meal and sauce mixture. Sprinkle bacon bits and grated mozzarella over the top.

13. Place the pumpkin, lid off, on the Weber griddle pan in the middle of the grid in the Weber and cook for 15 minutes.

14. Remove the pumpkin from the Weber and place it on a heat-resistant table mat. Cut it in generous slices and serve with the remaining warmed tomato mixture.

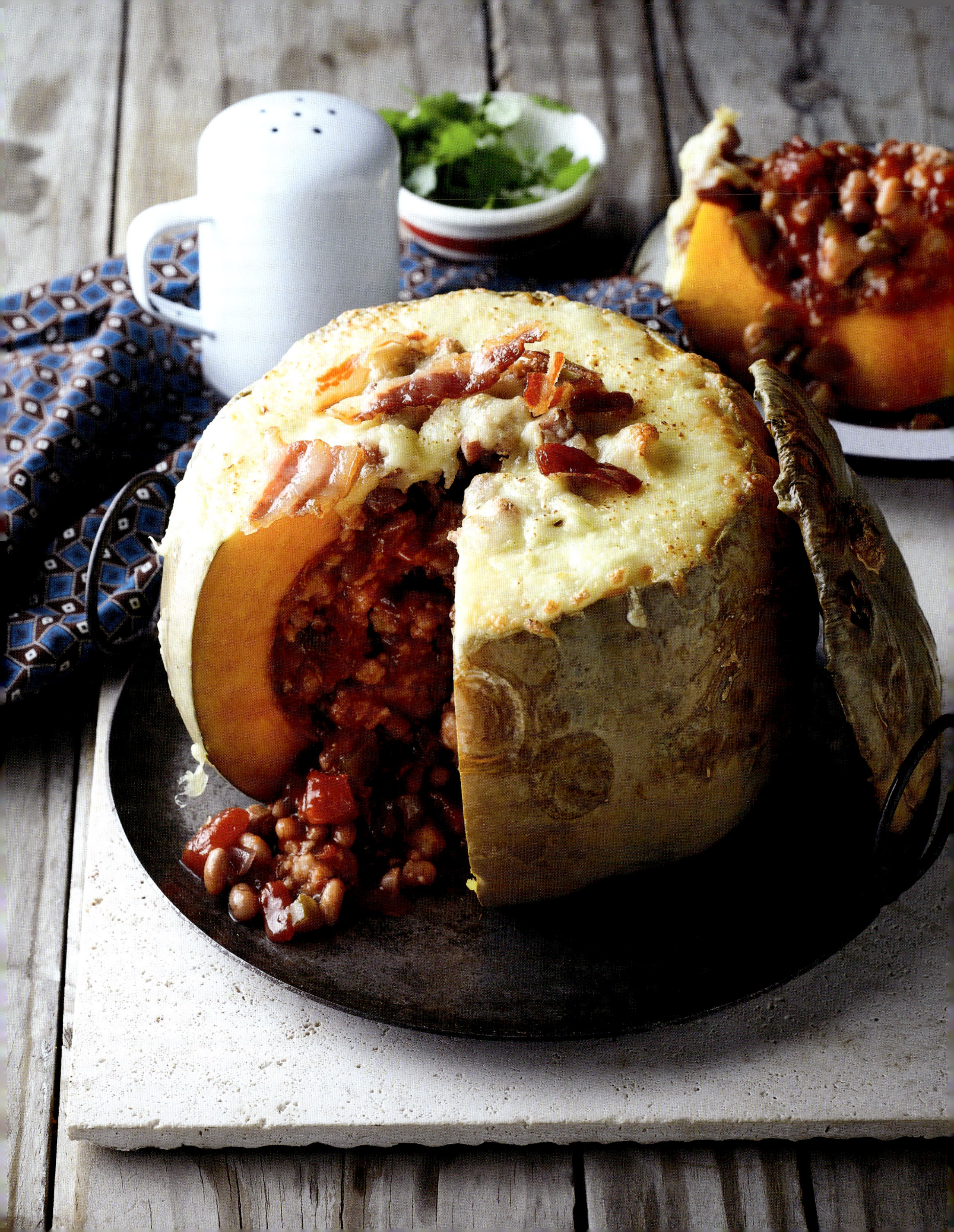

CHEESY BRAAI BOMB

A tempting and tasty addition to just about any snack platter!

Flour, for rolling
1 roll Today puff pastry
1 wheel President Camembert cheese
Wellington's sweet chilli sauce
1 egg
1 tbsp water

SPECIAL REQUIREMENTS
1 Weber kettle braai

1. Dust your work surface with flour and use a rolling pin to roll out the pastry.

2. Once rolled out, cut the pastry portion in half.

3. Place the Camembert cheese in the centre of the puff pastry and generously coat the Camembert wheel with sweet chilli sauce.

4. Wrap the pastry over the camembert corner to corner until it is completely encased in a puff pastry parcel.

5. Use the remaining puff pastry to create the pastry decorations. Cut out and score puff pastry strips with a knife to create leaf shapes. Roll a rectangular piece of puff pastry into a rose.

6. Mix the egg together with the water to make an egg wash. Brush the pastry parcel with the egg wash.

7. Place the decorations on the top of the parcel and brush with the egg wash.

8. Place the puff pastry parcel in the preheated Weber and bake slowly until golden brown.

9. Slice open to serve.

CHEESE AND ONION POTBROOD

Caramelised balsamic onions and two rounds of camembert baked inside a potbrood on the braai ... UNREAL!

2 cups lukewarm water
10 g instant dried yeast (1 packet)
4 cups Sasko white bread wheat flour
½ tsp salt
1 tbsp olive oil
2 onions, chopped
¾ cup brown sugar
¾ cup balsamic vinegar
Butter
2 whole Camembert cheese wheels

Deliciously decadent and dangerously moreish ...
– ALICIA WITTEN-RIDDLES

1. Pour 1 cup of lukewarm water into a mixing bowl. Add the instant yeast and set aside.

2. In a separate mixing bowl, combine the flour with the salt. Add the yeast mixture to the centre of the flour.

3. Combine the flour and yeast with a wooden spoon and add the remaining 1 cup of lukewarm water until you have a moist and kneadable dough.

4. Knead the dough for a few minutes. Then cover with a clean, dry dishcloth. Leave the dough to rise for about 30 minutes.

5. Heat the olive oil in a pan and brown the chopped onions with brown sugar and balsamic vinegar until caramelised.

6. Grease a small ovenproof pot with butter.

7. When the dough has doubled in size, knock it down into a flat disc.

8. Stack the Camembert wheels in the middle of the dough with the caremelised onion mixture in-between and gather the rest of the dough around the cheese, making a sort of pouch.

9. Pinch the dough to close the seams to stop the cheese from leaking out.

10. Put the bread in the pot with the seams facing down. Leave it to rise for about 20 minutes.

11. Bake over hot coals with a few embers on the lid for 45 minutes.

12. Remove the bread from the pot and allow to cool slightly before slicing.

BRAAI DAY SNACKS THREE WAYS

Three fuss-free, fail-proof snack ideas prepped on the braai. Your guests will love these!

DOUBLE CHEESE PIZZA PINWHEEL

1 roll Today puff pastry, defrosted
Flour for dusting
½ cup sun-dried tomato pesto
1 cup grated Parmalat cheddar cheese
1 cup grated Parmalat white cheddar cheese
1 pack streaky bacon, fried until crispy and cut into pieces
Fresh oregano

SPECIAL REQUIREMENTS
1 Weber kettle braai

1. Roll out the puff pastry using a rolling pin and a dusting of flour on the work surface.

2. Spread the sun-dried tomato pesto over the pastry.

3. Sprinkle half of the cheddar and half of the white cheddar over the pastry.

4. Sprinkle crispy bacon pieces and fresh oregano over the pastry.

5. Roll the pastry into a log and slice the log into 12–15 pinwheels.

6. Top each pinwheel with the remaining cheese, bacon pieces and fresh oregano.

7. Bake in the Weber until the pastry is cooked and the cheese is melted.

Thanks to this I am one of the best in the kitchen.
— LINDANI MCHUNU

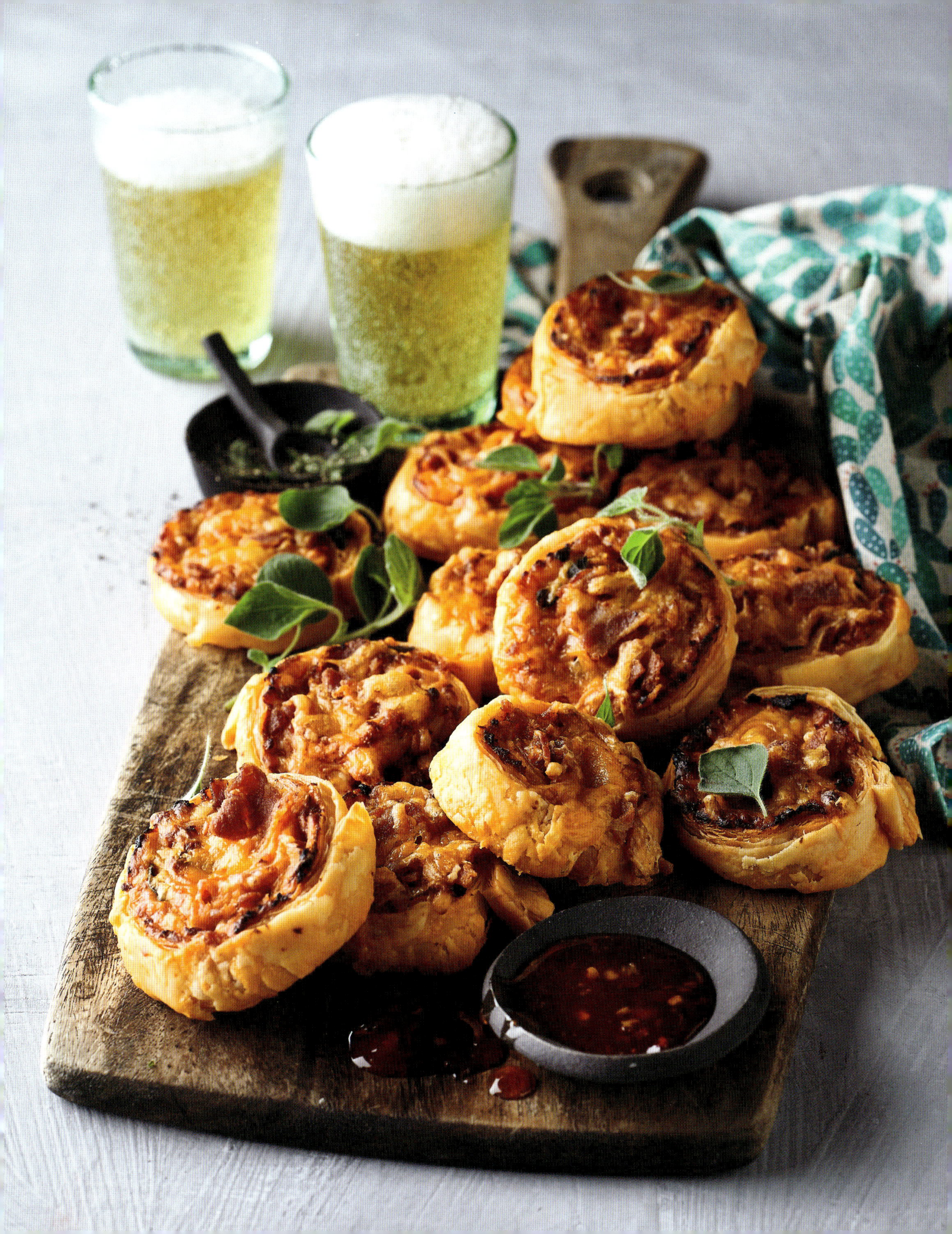

BRAAI DAY SNACKS THREE WAYS:
PIGS IN A BLANKET

4 pieces of boerewors, the length of the cheddar cheese slices
1 roll Today puff pastry
Flour for rolling
8 Parmalat cheddar cheese slices

SPECIAL REQUIREMENTS
1 Weber kettle braai
4 sosatie sticks, soaked in water before using

FOR SERVING
Sesame seeds (optional)
Dipping sauce of your choice

1. Cook the boerewors on soaked sosatie sticks to keep the pieces straight.

2. Allow the boerewors to cool once cooked.

3. Roll out the puff pastry on a dusting of flour. Cut the pastry into 4 rectangles.

4. Place 2 slices of cheddar cheese on each rectangle.

5. Top the cheese with a piece of the boerewors.

6. Roll up each pastry rectangle and slice each roll into smaller bite-sized pieces.

7. Bake in the Weber until the pastry is golden brown.

8. Garnish with sesame seeds if using and serve with a dipping sauce.

BRAAI DAY SNACKS THREE WAYS: CREAM CHEESE BILTONG BITES

1 roll Today puff pastry
Flour for rolling
6 tbsp Parmalat spring onion cream cheese
Biltong, thinly sliced
1 egg
1 tbsp water

1. Roll out the puff pastry using a rolling pin and a dusting of flour.

2. Using an empty, clean can, cut out circles in the pastry, 2 circles per biltong bite, so 12 in total.

3. Add 1 tbsp of spring onion cream cheese to 6 of the pastry rounds and top each with a few pieces of thinly sliced biltong.

4. Close the pocket with the second pastry round. Use a fork to press down the edges to seal the biltong bite.

5. Brush the pastry pockets with egg wash, made by mixing the egg and water.

6. Bake in the Weber until golden brown and serve.

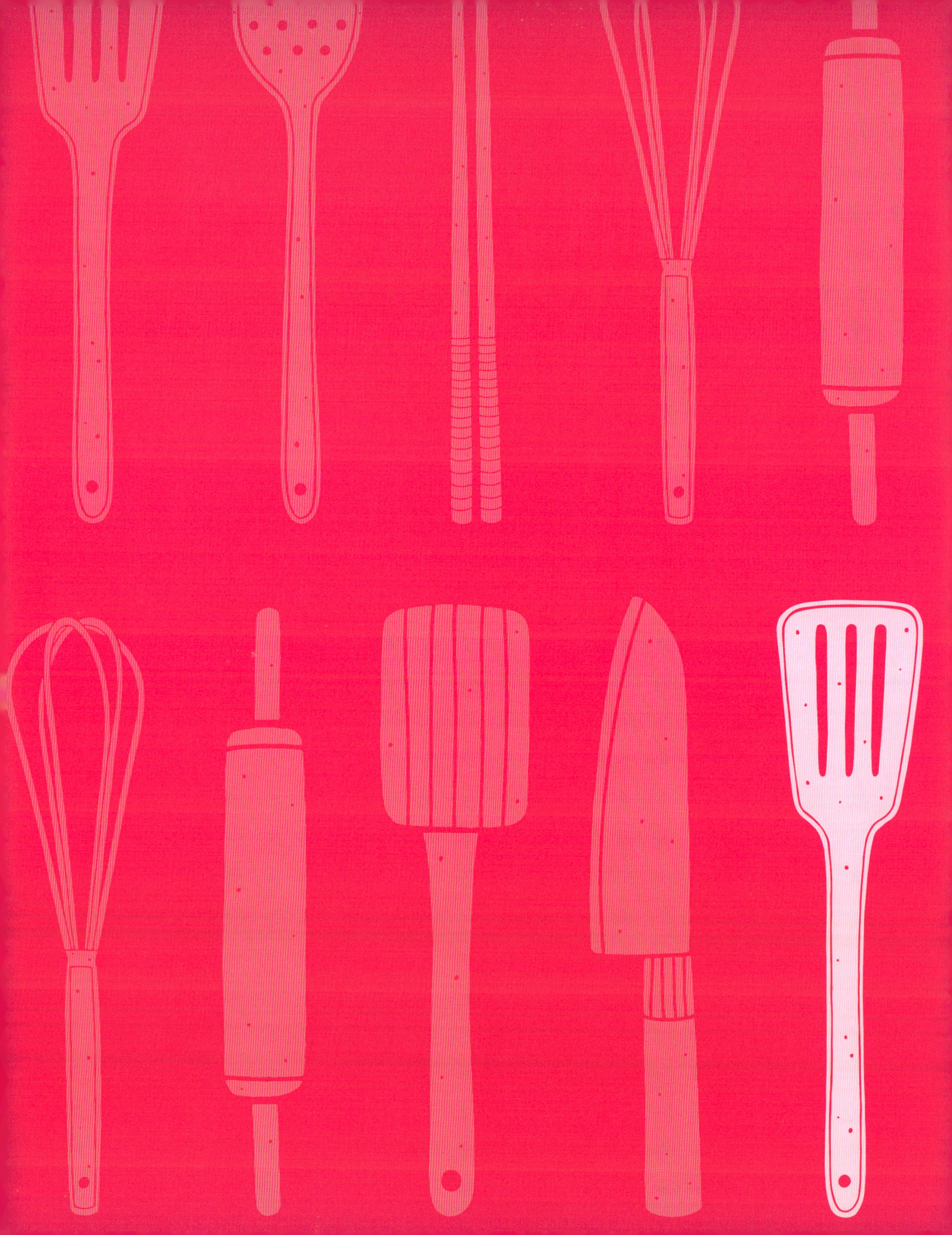

Sweet STUFF

Galaxy DONUTS

Ooo – these donuts are OUT OF THIS WORLD ... And they're actually far easier to make than you'd think!

FOR THE DONUTS
1 cup Sasko self-raising flour
⅓ cup caster sugar
⅓ cup buttermilk
3 tbsp butter, melted
1 egg

FOR THE ICING
1 cup icing sugar
5–8 tbsp cream
Moir's red and blue food colouring
Glitter sprinkles
Ribbons for serving

Fun factor **10**

1. Sift the self-raising flour into a mixing bowl. Once sifted add the caster sugar.

2. In a separate jug, whisk together the buttermilk, butter and egg. Add the wet ingredients to the dry and combine until smooth.

3. Pour the batter into a piping bag and pipe the mixture into a donut tray.

4. Bake the donuts at 200°C for 7–9 minutes.

5. For the icing, mix the icing sugar with the cream, adding just enough cream to achieve the desired consistency.

6. Once smooth, add drops of red and blue food colouring and stir in a figure-of-eight motion using a chopstick to create the galaxy icing effect.

7. Swirl the donuts through the icing to ice them with galaxy swirls.

8. Top with glitter sprinkles, loop ribbons through the donut centre and serve as donuts on a string.

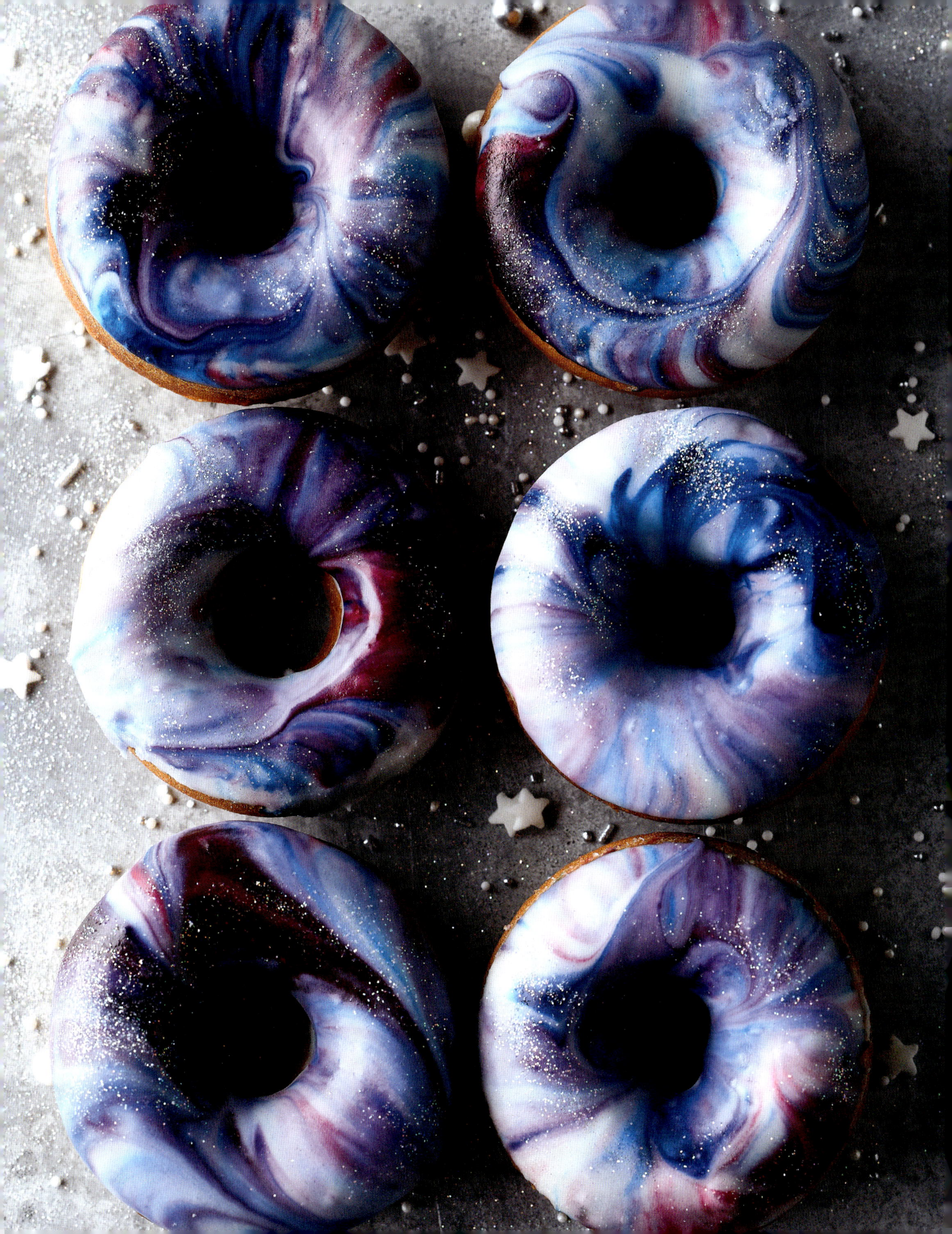

Frozen SMOOTHIE CAKE

Mmm ... This cake is so healthy you can eat it for breakfast!!

FOR THE GRANOLA LAYER
1½ cups Food Lover's honey and almond muesli
¼ cup shredded coconut
1 tbsp Food Lover's Market peanut butter
1 tbsp honey

FOR THE STRAWBERRY LAYER
1 cup strawberries
1 banana, sliced
¼ cup coconut cream

FOR THE BANANA LAYER
1 cup banana, sliced
1 cup Food Lover's Market double cream yoghurt

FOR THE BLUEBERRY LAYER
1 cup blueberries
1 cup banana, sliced
¼ cup coconut cream

TO GARNISH
Frozen blueberries
Frozen raspberries
Sliced strawberries
Fresh mint leaves

1. Make the granola layer by mixing the muesli with the shredded coconut, peanut butter and honey. Line a 23–25 cm diameter round cake tin with wax paper and spread the mixture into the bottom of the tin.

2. Place in the fridge to set.

3. In a blender, blitz the ingredients for the remaining three layers individually.

4. Pour the mixture for the strawberry layer into the tin and place in the freezer for at least 45 minutes to freeze.

5. Repeat with the other two layers.

6. The cake is ready as soon as the top layer is hard, but you can keep it in the freezer as long as you like.

7. Slice the cake while still frozen and serve with berries and mint leaves to garnish.

Amarula CHEESECAKE

A creamy, dreamy Amarula cheesecake that tastes heavenly!

FOR THE BASE
200g digestive biscuits
½ cup melted butter

FOR THE CHEESECAKE
1½ cups Amarula cream liqueur
1 tbsp gelatin
500g cream cheese
½ cup sugar
2 cups cream

FOR THE TOPPING
Caramel popcorn
Chocolate pretzels
Honeycomb pieces

1. For the base, crush the digestive biscuits. Add the melted butter to the biscuits and mix to combine. Spread the biscuit mixture evenly at the bottom of a standard size cake tin (23–25 cm diameter) and press flat with a spoon. Freeze for 10 minutes.

2. In a separate bowl, combine 1 cup of the Amarula with gelatin and microwave for 1 minute, until the gelatin is melted. Allow to cool.

3. In a large mixing bowl, combine the cream cheese with the sugar and mix using a hand-held mixer until light and fluffy.

4. Add the Amarula and gelatin mixture to the cream cheese and beat with the hand-held mixer until combined.

5. Beat the cream until light and fluffy and add half of the whipped cream to the cream cheese mixture.

6. Spread the mixture over the biscuit base and refrigerate for 2 hours.

7. Remove the cheesecake from the tin and top with caramel popcorn, chocolate pretzels, honeycomb pieces and dollops of the remaining Amarula cream.

8. Slice and serve.

I just licked my phone!
– LINDA ANDREW

Delish!

Peanut Butter
STUFFED CHOCOLATE FLAPJACKS

Chocolate flapjacks + a melted peanut butter centre = all kinds of DELICIOUS!

FOR THE FLAPJACKS
- 10 tsp peanut butter
- 2 eggs
- 2½ cups milk
- ¼ cup oil
- 1⅓ cup flour
- ⅔ cup White Star chocolate-flavour instant maize porridge
- 2 tbsp sugar
- 4 tsp baking powder
- 1 tsp salt
- ¼ cup cocoa powder
- Oil for frying

TO SERVE
- Honey
- Banana slices
- Strawberries (optional)
- Icing sugar for dusting

1. Line a baking sheet with wax paper. Using a teaspoon to measure, make 10 peanut butter balls and space them evenly on the sheet.

2. Using a butter knife, spread and flatten the peanut butter balls so that they look like flattened saucers, about 4 cm in diameter.

3. Freeze for 4 hours.

4. In a large bowl, whisk the eggs, milk and oil.

5. In a separate bowl, combine the flour, chocolate instant maize porridge, sugar, baking powder, salt and cocoa powder.

6. Stir the wet ingredients into the dry ingredients just until moistened.

7. Pour ¼ cup of batter into an oiled pan, then immediately place one of the frozen peanut butter circles onto the batter.

8. Spoon about 3 tablespoons of batter on top of the peanut butter to cover it completely. Flip and fry the other side of the flapjack until cooked through.

9. Continue to make 10 flapjacks in this way.

10. Serve the flapjacks stacked and topped with honey, banana slices, strawberries (if using) and a dusting of icing sugar.

Layered Chocolate RICE PUDDING

A whole new way to think about rice!

FOR THE LAYERS
¼ cup coconut
¼ cup chia seeds
¾ cup coconut milk
½ cup coconut water
1 tsp vanilla essence
⅓ cup Tastic basmati rice
3¼ cups milk
¼ cup cocoa powder
¼ cup caster sugar
2 ripe bananas

FOR THE GARNISH
Almonds
Coconut
Cocoa powder

1. Place the coconut and chia seeds in a mason jar with the coconut milk and coconut water and stir to combine. Add the vanilla essence and refrigerate for 2 hours.

2. While the chia seed pudding is setting, rinse the basmati rice under water. Place the rinsed rice in a pot with 3 cups of the milk.

3. In a separate bowl, combine the cocoa powder with the remaining ¼ cup of milk. Once mixed, add to the pot.

4. Add the caster sugar to the pot, mix and bring to the boil. Reduce the heat and cook for 35 minutes with the lid on.

5. Remove the lid and cook for a further 10 minutes.

6. Mash the ripe bananas using a fork.

7. Assemble the puddings in a glass, starting with a layer of chocolate rice pudding, then mashed banana followed by chia seed pudding on top.

8. Garnish with almonds, coconut and cocoa powder and serve.

Peanut Butter Cookie S'mores Pizza

A peanut butter cookie base + a silky smooth chocolate layer + perfectly roasted marshmallows = the sweetest, stickiest, most delicious dessert pizza you will ever eat!

FOR THE PEANUT BUTTER COOKIE
- 1 cup unsalted butter
- 1 cup crunchy peanut butter
- 1 cup white sugar
- 1 cup packed brown sugar
- 2 eggs
- 2½ cups Sasko cake flour
- 1 tsp baking powder
- 1½ tsp bicarbonate of soda
- ½ tsp salt

FOR THE GANACHE AND TOPPINGS
- 1 cup heavy cream
- 1⅓ cup chocolate, broken into pieces
- 1 bag of white marshmallows

1. Cream the butter, peanut butter and sugars together in a bowl. Beat in the eggs.

2. In a separate bowl, sift the flour, baking powder, bicarbonate of soda and salt. Stir into the peanut butter cookie mixture. Wrap the dough in plastic and refrigerate for 1 hour.

3. Roll out the dough and place it on a pizza tray or baking sheet.

4. Bake at 180 °C for 20 minutes or until the cookie begins to brown.

5. Allow to cool.

6. Bring heavy cream to a simmer on the stove top, stirring occasionally. Just as soon as you see a simmer, remove from heat and pour over chocolate pieces in a bowl, swirling the bowl to make sure all of the chocolate is covered.

7. Swirl the chocolate with a whisk starting in the centre and working outward until smooth.

8. Spread the ganache over the peanut butter cookie.

9. Slice marshmallows in half so that they are not as tall. Place the marshmallows sliced-side down on the chocolate and cover the cookie completely.

10. Place in the oven at 180 °C. Watch carefully so that it doesn't burn and remove as soon as the marshmallows begin to brown.

11. Slice into wedges and serve.

Drool button please, Facebook.
– NATALIE ELLIOT

Marshmallow AND POPCORN SQUARES

Fun factor 10

Crunchy, chewy, colourful *and* tasty! These squares are the ultimate party treat and they're incredibly easy to make.

2 tbsp oil
½ cup Imbo popcorn
50 g Bokomo Otees
1 cup Smarties
100 g Safari raw cashews
⅓ cup butter
300 g marshmallows

1. Add the oil and popcorn kernels to the pot and close the lid.
2. Pop over high heat (be sure to be attentive to popcorn to avoid letting it burn).
3. Pour the popcorn into a large mixing bowl.
4. Add the Otees, Smarties and cashews to the bowl.
5. Melt the butter in a pot over low to medium heat.
6. When the butter is melted, add the marshmallows and mix together with a wooden spoon until liquefied into a runny, sticky mixture. Keep stirring to prevent the mixture sticking to the bottom of the pot.
7. Pour the marshmallow mixture into the mixing bowl with the popcorn, Otees, Smarties and raw cashews. Mix together well.
8. Pour the mixture into a 20 × 25 cm glass tray lined with wax paper. Pat down and flatten the mixture, making sure to fill up the entire glass tray.
9. Allow to set for 20 minutes.
10. Remove from the tray, cut into even-sized squares and serve.

Kid-friendly!

Red Velvet
ICE CREAM CONE CUPCAKES

Is it an ice cream? Is it a cupcake? IT'S BOTH ... YUM!

FOR THE CUPCAKES
1 cup milk
1 cup oil
2 large eggs
Sasko Quick Treats vanilla muffin mix
Moir's crimson pink food colouring
8 flat-bottomed ice cream cones

FOR THE ICING
Cream cheese
Caster sugar

FOR THE GARNISH
Chocolate sprinkles
Flaked almonds
Silver sugar balls
Funfetti

1. Preheat the oven to 180 °C.

2. Pour the milk and oil into a large mixing bowl.

3. Add the eggs and mix until combined.

4. Add the vanilla muffin mix to the bowl and stir until the batter is smooth.

5. Add the food colouring to the batter and stir.

6. Using a knife, cut holes into the base of a disposable aluminium baking tray.

7. Place the ice cream cones upright in the holes.

8. Using a piping bag or a spoon, pipe the cupcake batter into each ice cream cone. Make sure not to fill it right to the top – leave space for it to rise.

9. Place the aluminium tray into the oven. Bake for 25 minutes.

10. In a separate bowl, combine the cream cheese and caster sugar, stirring until smooth.

11. Remove the cupcakes from the oven and allow to cool for 10 minutes.

12. Spread the icing over the cupcakes and garnish with chocolate sprinkles, flaked almonds, silver sugar balls and funfetti.

French Toast WAFFLES

The simplicity of waffles + the taste of French toast = a genius dessert (or breakfast) idea!

FOR THE FRENCH TOAST WAFFLES
2 tbsp butter, melted
2 eggs
½ cup milk
½ tsp Moir's vanilla essence
¼ tsp cinnamon
4 slices Sasko Low GI all-in-one bread

FOR SERVING
Maple syrup
Raspberries, to garnish

1. Preheat a waffle iron and brush both sides of the waffle iron with melted butter to prevent sticking.
2. Whisk the eggs, milk, vanilla essence and cinnamon in a bowl until frothy.
3. Dip the bread slices into the egg mixture briefly and flip each slice to coat both sides.
4. Place the dipped bread slices into the heated waffle iron and cook until golden brown.
5. Serve with a drizzle of maple syrup and a handful of raspberries.

BRILLIANT – WHO WOULD'VE THOUGHT OF MAKING FRENCH TOAST IN THE WAFFLE MAKER!

Farm-Style APPLE PIES

A flop-proof dessert idea that your friends and family will love!

FOR THE APPLE PIES
6 Granny Smith apples
1 cup Ceres apple fruit juice (add more juice as needed)
3 tbsp sugar
½ tsp cinnamon
About ¼ pack of puff pastry
Flour for rolling
1 egg
1 tbsp water
1 tbsp brown sugar

FOR SERVING
Ice cream for serving
Maple syrup

1. Cut off the top of 4 apples.

2. Remove the inside of each apple very carefully with a spoon or fruit baller, making sure not to puncture the peel.

3. Peel and cut the 2 remaining apples into pieces. Add all the apple pieces (without the seeds) to a saucepan with the apple juice, sugar and cinnamon.

4. Bring to the boil and allow to simmer until sticky and caramelised.

5. Scoop the caramelised apple mixture into the hollow apples.

6. Roll out the puff pastry with flour and slice into strips.

7. Cover the top of the apples in a lattice pattern with puff pastry strips.

8. Brush the puff pastry strips with egg wash (make it with the egg and water) and a sprinkling of brown sugar.

9. Add a dash of water to the bottom of the baking pan, just enough to cover the bottom (this will prevent the apples from drying out while baking).

10. Place the apple pies in the baking dish. Cover with foil and bake at 180°C for 25 minutes or until the crust is golden brown and the apples are soft.

11. Slice open and serve with a dollop of ice cream and a drizzle of maple syrup.

Well, now here is a new way of making apple pie. I must try this method!
– BRUCE BOWERS

156 | SWEET STUFF

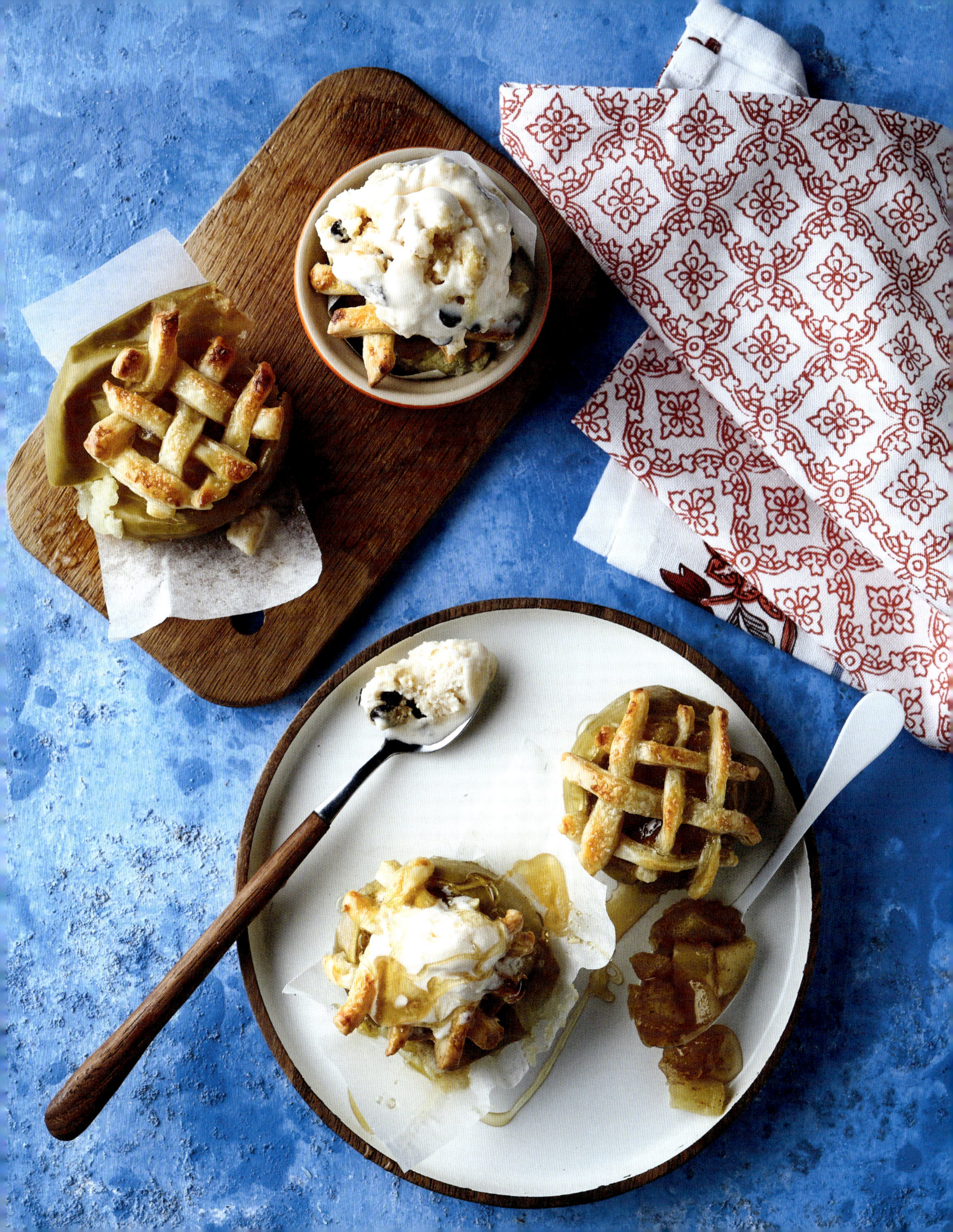

Apple Flapjacks

Basically like an apple pie, but in flapjack form – gotta love it!

FOR THE APPLE FLAPJACKS
2 apples
½ tsp Food Lover's cinnamon, and more for dusting
2 tbsp butter, melted
1 tbsp vanilla essence
1 egg
¾ cup Food Lover's milk
1 cup flour
2 tbsp baking powder
Food Lover's extra virgin olive oil for frying

FOR SERVING
1 can caramel treat
Whipped cream
Honey, for garnishing

1. Using a potato peeler, peel the apples.
2. Cut the apples into 2 cm-thick slices.
3. Using a melon baller, remove the apple core from each apple slice.
4. Sprinkle a dusting of cinnamon over the apple slices.
5. In a separate bowl, whisk the melted butter, vanilla, egg and milk.
6. Sift the flour and baking powder into the mixture. Add half a teaspoon of cinnamon and mix.
7. Dip the apple slices in the flapjack mixture, coating both sides.
8. Fry the apple flapjacks in olive oil until golden brown.
9. Serve the flapjacks in a stack, layered with caramel treat and topped with whipped cream, a drizzle of honey and a dusting of cinnamon.

Second time watching this suddenly makes it look twice as nice!
– LEIGH VAN DER BERGH

Banana Fritters WITH TOFFEE SAUCE

A sweet and sticky snack or dessert option that will leave you licking your fingers – for sure!

FOR THE TOFFEE SAUCE
½ cup butter
½ cup sugar
½ cup thick cream
½ tsp vanilla essence

FOR THE BANANA FRITTERS
¼ cup White Star banana-flavour instant maize porridge
1 cup all-purpose flour
1 tsp baking powder
¼ tsp bicarbonate of soda
Pinch of salt
1 large egg
1 tsp vanilla essence
1 tsp lemon juice
2 bananas, roughly chopped
Vegetable oil, for frying
Icing sugar (optional), for dusting

1. For the toffee sauce, melt the butter in a saucepan together with the sugar, thick cream and vanilla essence.

2. Bring to the boil and set aside once caramelised.

3. For the banana fritters, combine the instant maize porridge with the all-purpose flour, baking powder, bicarbonate of soda and salt in a large mixing bowl. Whisk to combine.

4. Whisk the egg, vanilla essence and lemon juice in a separate bowl.

5. Add the wet ingredients to the dry ingredients along with the chopped banana and use a spatula to fold the mixture together until just combined.

6. Use a spoon to gently drop spoonfuls of batter into the hot oil and fry on one side until the edges start to turn golden brown.

7. Flip and continue frying until golden brown on the other side.

8. Drain and let the fritters cool a bit before dusting with icing sugar.

9. Serve warm with the toffee sauce.

Wow, everything is mouthwatering, I don't know which one to try first.
– LINDA SIBEKO

Dreamy!

160 | SWEET STUFF

Peppermint Crisp
TRIFLE CUPS

This easy-to-make dessert idea features custard and other South African favourites!

FOR THE CAKE
1 pack of chocolate cake mix with the necessary ingredients
Butter and flour

FOR THE TRIFLE CUPS (MAKES 4)
1 can caramel treat
2 cups Parmalat custard
3 × 49 g Peppermint Crisp chocolate bars
1 cup whipped cream
4 mason jars for assembling
Caramel sauce for serving

1. For the cake, preheat the oven to 180 °C.

2. Prepare the cake batter according to the instructions on the pack.

3. Grease a rectangular baking tin with butter and dust with flour. Pour in the cake batter to make a layer about 1 cm thick.

4. Bake for 25–30 minutes, remove from the oven and allow to cool.

5. Use a mason jar as a cookie cutter to create round cut-outs of the cake. These will be used as the cake layers in your trifles.

6. To assemble the trifle cups, add a spoonful of caramel to the bottom of each jar and top with a slice of cake. Add a layer of the custard.

7. Crumble Peppermint Crisp over the custard.

8. Add a second slice of cake on top of the crumbled Peppermint Crisp and top with more caramel, custard, a dollop of whipped cream and more crushed Peppermint Crisp.

9. Drizzle with caramel sauce before serving. NOTE: Make the caramel sauce by heating some of the caramel.

Froyo FRUIT CONES

A fun, frozen and fruity snack idea for carefree summer days!

80 g slab milk chocolate
100 g Food Lover's Market hazelnuts
4 ice cream cones
3 cups Food Lover's Market double cream yoghurt
3 tbsp Food Lover's Market honey
Strawberries
Kiwis
Gooseberries
Blueberries
Nectarines
Honey to drizzle

1. Roughly chop the milk chocolate slab and melt it over a bowl of boiling water until smooth.

2. Use a rolling pin to crush the hazelnuts in the packet.

3. Dip the ice cream cones into the melted chocolate before rolling each cone in the crushed hazelnuts. Use a spoon to drizzle a dollop of chocolate into the bottom of each cone.

4. Place the cones into the fridge to set.

5. Mix the double cream yoghurt with the honey.

6. Spoon the yoghurt mixture into a piping bag and freeze for 1 hour.

7. Slice the fruit.

8. Pipe the frozen yoghurt into the cones and top with an assortment of the fruit.

9. Top with a drizzle of honey before serving.

These look amazing!!!
— JORDYNS CHANNEL

Yummm 😍😍😍😍
— THE SIHLE NDABA

Froyo Sarmies

Creamy yoghurt blended with fresh berries and frozen between two crunchy biscuit layers = a healthier take on the much loved ice-cream sandwich!

18 square biscuits
3 cups Parmalat double cream yoghurt
1 tbsp honey
1½ cups blueberries
1½ cups strawberries

1. Line a square baking tin with baking paper. Place 9 square biscuits at the base of the pan so that there are no gaps.

2. In a small bowl, mix together 1 cup of the double cream yoghurt and the honey.

3. Spread the yoghurt and honey mixture evenly over the biscuits and place in the freezer for about 1 hour to set.

4. Blend 1 cup of the blueberries with 1 cup double cream yoghurt until a smooth consistency is achieved.

5. Remove the baking tin from the freezer and pour the blueberry mixture over the honey and yoghurt layer. Drop a few whole blueberries into the layer before placing in the freezer for 1 hour to set.

6. Repeat the blending process with 1 cup of the chopped strawberries and 1 cup double cream yoghurt.

7. Remove the tin from the freezer and pour the strawberry mixture over the set blueberry layer. Chop the remaining ½ cup of strawberries and add some to the layer before freezing.

8. While the mixture is still a bit sticky, place the final layer of square biscuits over the top and freeze for a while longer.

9. Remove from the freezer, top with any remaining berries, slice and serve.

Again with the food sorcery, Foodies of SA!
– NDIVHUWO MULAUDZI

SWEET STUFF

Brownie Bowls

What's better than licking the bowl?! EATING IT! These loaded 'bowls' are perfect for parties, cheat days; or just as a fun weekend baking project!

FOR THE BROWNIES
200 g baking chocolate
150 g butter
1 x 500 g packet Sasko cookie mix
¼ cup cocoa
3 eggs
1 tsp vanilla essence

FOR SERVING
Vanilla ice cream
Candied cherries
80 g slab milk chocolate
100s & 1000s coloured sprinkles

1. Half fill a small saucepan with water and bring to the boil, reduce to a simmer and place a glass mixing bowl over the saucepan.

2. Add baking chocolate and butter to this bowl and stir slowly until completely melted.

3. Pour the cookie mix into a separate bowl. Add cocoa, beaten eggs and vanilla essence to the bowl. Top with melted chocolate and mix until smooth.

4. Spray a standard 12-cup muffin tin with cooking spray and scoop the brownie mixture into each cup until about ⅔ full. Bake at 180 °C for 20 minutes, or until a skewer inserted into the centre comes out clean.

5. Once the brownies are baked, remove from the oven and immediately press either a glass jar or bottle, or the underside of a second muffin tin, into the brownies to create hollows. Allow to cool.

6. Repeat the chocolate melting process performed earlier, using the slab of milk chocolate.

7. Once melted, drizzle the melted chocolate over the brownie cups and top with ice cream and toppings of choice.

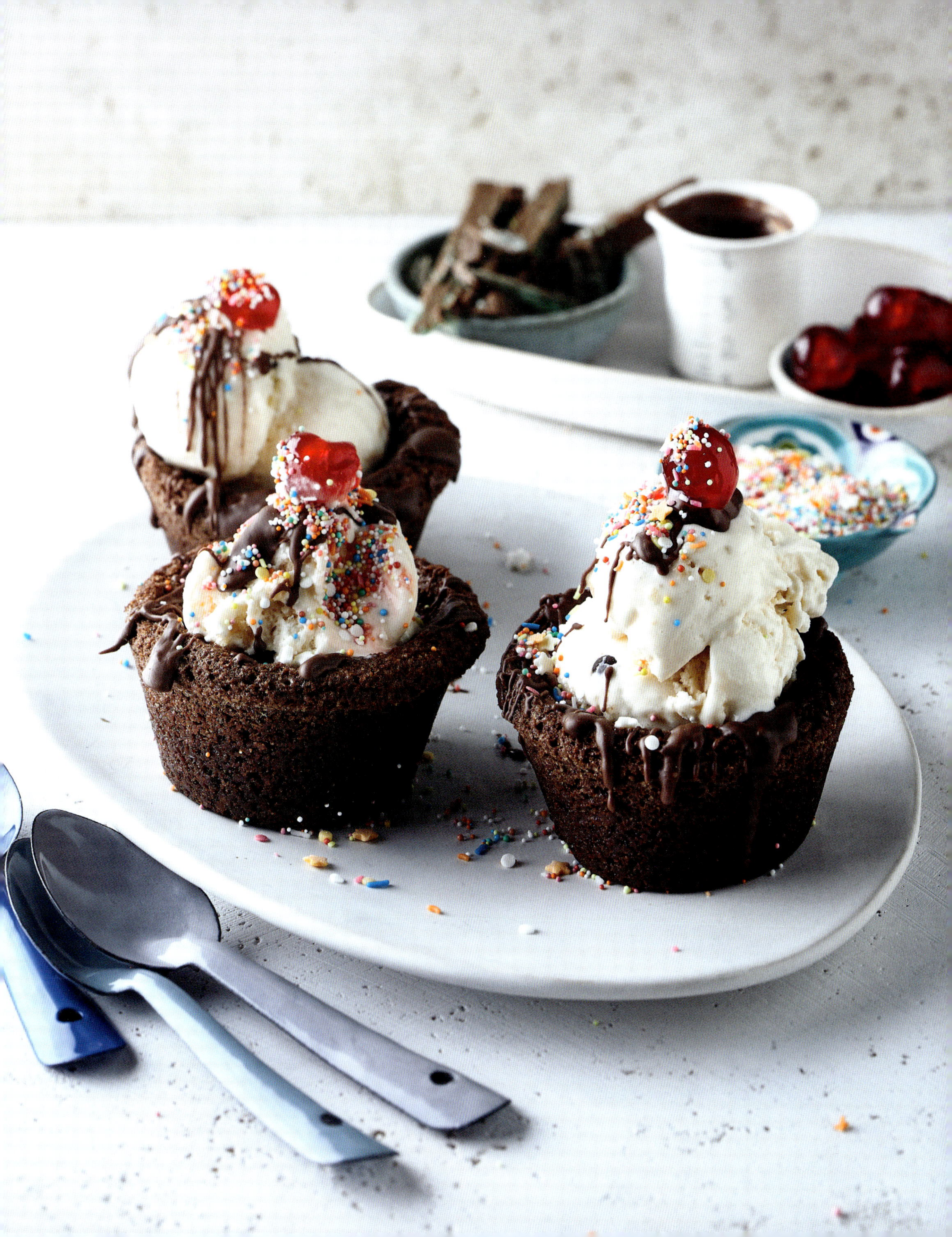

Warm WHISKY VOLCANO

A totally irresistible flaming chocolate dessert with a silky, molten centre …
This is guaranteed to blow your guests away!

FOR THE CHOCOLATE DESSERTS
150 g dark chocolate
150 g butter
85 g sugar
Pinch of salt
3 eggs
3 egg yolks
1 shot Three Ships Bourbon Cask Finish whisky
1 tbsp flour
Butter for greasing
Cocoa powder for dusting

FOR SERVING
4 shots Three Ships Bourbon Cask Finish whisky

1. Melt dark chocolate together with butter and sugar in a bowl over boiling water.
2. Once melted, add a pinch of salt and stir to combine.
3. Remove from the heat and whisk the 3 eggs as well as the 3 egg yolks into the mixture.
4. Add 1 shot of Three Ships whisky to the mixture together with the flour and stir to combine.
5. Preheat the oven to 200 °C.
6. Grease the sides and base of 4 baking ramekins with butter. Once coated, add a dusting of cocoa powder into each.
7. Pour the chocolate and whisky mixture into the ramekins and bake for 10–12 minutes.
8. Remove from the oven and flip the ramekins over so that the chocolate volcano can slide out.
9. Top each with a shot of whisky and fire them up for the flambé.
10. Serve immediately.

I'm dead! 😂😂😂😂😂
– GUGU GUMEDE

5-MINUTE Mug Cake

Quick, easy and divine – perfect for lazy days or evenings curled up on the couch!

2 tbsp butter
2 bars of Aero Duet/Aero Peppermint (40 g for cooking, 25 g melted, 20 g crushed)
1 egg
4 tbsp flour
½ tsp baking powder
1 pinch of salt
1 tsp cocoa powder
½ tsp vanilla essence
Vanilla ice cream (optional)

1. Place the butter and 40 g Aero chocolate in a microwave-proof mug. Melt the butter and chocolate on high in the microwave for 40 seconds. Then mix well.

2. Beat the egg and add it to the melted chocolate mixture.

3. Add the flour, baking powder, salt, cocoa powder and vanilla essence and stir until combined.

4. Place the mug in the microwave and cook on high for 2 minutes.

5. Remove the mug from the microwave and let it sit for a few minutes to cool.

6. Top the cake with ice cream, 25 g melted Aero and 20 g crushed Aero pieces.

7. Grab a spoon and dig in.

SWEET STUFF

Rainbow POPSICLES

Deliciously refreshing treats, packed with goodness, colour and creativity. Rope in your kids to help you make these!

1 cup blueberries
1 cup kiwi fruit, cut into quarters
1 cup orange segments, halved
1 cup cubed pineapple
1 cup strawberries
1 ⅗ cup Liqui-Fruit clear apple juice
1 ⅗ cup Liqui-Fruit mango and orange juice
⅘ cup Liqui-Fruit berry blaze juice

Fun factor **10**

1. Chop the blueberries, kiwi fruit quarters, orange segments, cubed pineapple and strawberries into small pieces.

2. Place all the fruit pieces on a tray and freeze. Keep each type of fruit separate on the tray.

3. Place the frozen blueberries into a blender together with half of the clear apple juice. Blend until smooth.

4. Spoon the mixture into the bottom of each hole in the popsicle mould and freeze until set. You will need about 8 moulds.

5. Blend the frozen kiwi fruit pieces with the remaining clear apple juice, layer the mixture over the first layer and return to the freezer to set.

6. Blend the frozen orange segments with half of the mango and orange juice. Spoon the mixture into the moulds as the third layer.

7. Blend the frozen pineapple with the remaining mango and orange juice. Spoon the mixture into the moulds as the fourth layer.

8. Blend the frozen strawberries with the berry blaze juice and spoon the mixture into the mould as the fifth and last layer.

9. Freeze until all layers have set and serve.

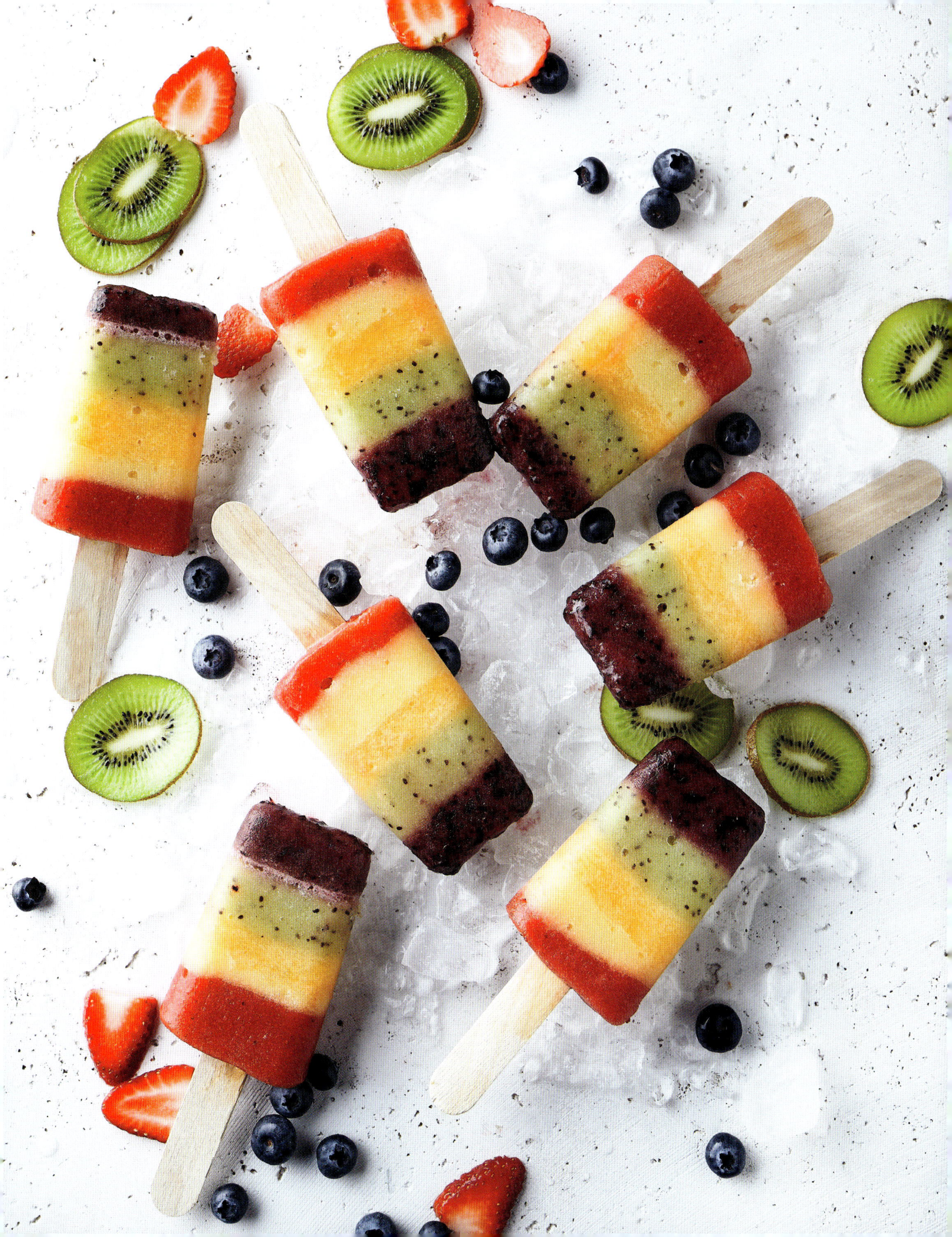

THREE-INGREDIENT HOME-MADE
Fruit Juice Pastilles

Healthy home-made sweet treats that will tempt the whole family!

4 cups Ceres fruit juice – flavour of your choosing
6 tbsp gelatin
3 cups sugar
Sugar for rolling

1. Add 1½ cups of the fruit juice and the gelatin to a pot, set aside and allow the gelatin to dissolve.
2. In a separate pot, bring the remaining 2½ cups fruit juice to the boil.
3. Once the juice has come to the boil, remove the pot from the heat.
4. Place the pot containing the gelatin mixture on the stove at medium heat.
5. Add the boiling juice to the gelatin mixture. Stir until combined over a medium heat.
6. Add the sugar to the pot, stirring until dissolved.
7. Boil for 25 minutes, stirring constantly. Remove the pot from the heat.
8. Prepare a rubber ice cube tray by spraying it with cooking spray.
9. Let the mixture cool before pouring it into the tray. Use a knife to spread the mixture evenly in the ice cube tray.
10. Chill for 4 hours or overnight.
11. Remove the pastilles from the ice cube tray and roll each pastille in sugar.
12. Allow the pastilles to dry on a rack or on paper towels before serving.

Home-made FRUIT ROLLS

These fruit rolls are a good lunchbox treat or on-the-go snack ...
Bonus: they are really easy to make!

2 cups Ceres Secrets of the Valley fruit juice
3 cups mixed berries
1 tsp freshly-squeezed lemon juice

1. Simmer the fruit juice for 15 minutes to reduce.

2. Blend together the berries and the freshly-squeezed lemon juice.

3. Add the juice reduction to the blended mixture and blend until smooth.

4. Strain the mixture to remove any lumps.

5. Pour the mixture onto a tray lined with baking paper and spread it out evenly.

6. Bake at 75 °C for 3½–4 hours.

7. Cut the fruit rolls into strips with the baking paper still attached.

8. Roll up the strips and keep each in place with a piece of string.

ICE CREAM *Sandwich*

A creamy ice cream layer sandwiched between two home-made cookies, dipped in melted chocolate and finished off with toppings of choice. Yum!

1 packet Sasko cookie mix
140 g butter
100 g chocolate chips
1 extra-large egg
3 cups vanilla ice cream, slightly softened

FOR THE GARNISH
Melted chocolate
Sprinkles
Crushed chips
Mini marshmallows

1. In a large bowl, combine the Sasko cookie mix with butter, using your fingers.

2. Add the chocolate chips and mix through.

3. Whisk the egg in a bowl before adding to the mixture.

4. Mix together until blended and remove ½ cup of the cookie dough for use later.

5. Using an ice cream scoop, scoop the remaining cookie dough onto a lined baking tray and press down on each dough ball to flatten it into a cookie shape for baking. You should get 12 cookies.

6. Bake at 180 °C for 12 minutes.

7. Mix the remaining ½ cup cookie dough with the vanilla ice cream. Place in the freezer if not using immediately.

8. Place the baked cookies bottom-side up and add a scoop of the cookie and ice cream mixture before covering with a second cookie and pressing down to make an ice cream sandwich.

9. Dip each ice cream sandwich in melted chocolate and coat with sprinkles, chips or mini marshmallows to garnish.

Count me in!

AERO DEEP-FRIED
Ice Cream

The perfect mix of creamy, crunchy and cool ... SO GOOD!

135 g slab Aero peppermint chocolate
135 g slab Aero milk chocolate
4 cups vanilla ice cream
1 egg
¼ teaspoon vanilla essence
¾ cups crushed cornflakes
Oil, for frying

1. Chop each Aero slab into pieces.

2. Divide the ice cream into 2 bowls and mix the peppermint Aero into one bowl and the milk chocolate Aero into the other (reserve a few pieces of milk chocolate to melt and drizzle over before serving and a few pieces of peppermint to crumble over the top).

3. Using an ice cream scoop, scoop balls of the mixture onto a cold baking sheet lined with baking paper.

4. Cover and freeze for at least 1 hour.

5. In one small bowl, whisk the egg and vanilla essence.

6. Place the crushed cornflakes in another small bowl.

7. Dip scoops of ice cream into the egg mixture and then roll them in the crushed cornflakes until they are evenly coated. Repeat once more before freezing the balls.

8. Heat oil in a large pot.

9. Deep-fry each ice cream ball for 12–15 seconds or until golden. Drain on paper towels.

10. Serve drizzled with melted milk chocolate Aero and crumble peppermint Aero over the top.

DEEP-FRIED ICE CREAM
— SA Style

Deep-fried ice cream taken to a new level with SA-style biscuits!

3 big scoops vanilla ice cream
6 Boudoir biscuits
12 Tennis biscuits
Half a bag Nuttikrust biscuits
1 egg, beaten
Oil, for frying

1. Use an ice cream scoop to scoop round ice cream balls. Try get them as perfectly round as possible.

2. Crush the biscuits together and roll each ice cream ball in the crushed biscuits until each ice cream ball is completely coated.

3. Place the ice cream balls in the freezer for at least 40 minutes.

4. Take the ice cream balls out of the freezer and roll them in egg before rolling them in the crushed biscuits a second time.

5. Place the ice cream balls in the freezer again and freeze until solid.

6. Heat oil in a pot until you can see oil lines appear.

7. Deep-fry the ice cream balls for 5–8 seconds until golden brown.

8. Serve immediately after frying.

Chocolate House

2–3 × 80 g Beacon milk chocolate slabs, to melt and use as glue
4 × 80 g Beacon mint slabs, for the base of the house
8 × 80 g Beacon milk chocolate slabs, for the front, back and sides of the house
6 × 80 g Beacon ebony and ivory chocolate slabs, for the roof, doors and windows

4 Beacon milk Wonder bars
Jelly Tots
Beacon Fav'rites
Beacon Allsorts
Maynards Starlight sweets
Jelly Tots, craziberries flavoured

1. In a bowl placed over a pot of boiling water, melt the milk chocolate slabs for the glue. Pour the melted chocolate into a piping bag.

2. For the base, use an (approximately) A4-sized board or thick card covered with foil or paper of your choice. In more or less the centre of the board, lay the four mint chocolate slabs horizontally, one next to the other to form the base. Use melted chocolate to glue the slabs together so that they don't move around.

3. Cut the rounded edges of the 8 milk chocolate slabs so that they're straight and glue together 2 vertical slabs each for the front and back and 2 horizontal slabs for the sides.

4. Once dry, lay the front section on a separate board. Count upwards 5 from the bottom and then, using a heating knife, cut each side (diagonally) at a 45° angle to form the triangular sections to hold up the roof. (NOTE: Refer to the photo.)

5. Repeat with the back section of the house.

6. Using melted chocolate glue, stand the front piece up on the base and glue one edge of the side pieces to each edge.

7. Then glue the back piece to the other edges of the sides. Make sure they fit together tightly. NOTE: Be patient and allow the chocolate glue to harden completely, to create a solid house.

8. For the roof, take 4 slabs of the ebony and ivory chocolate and cut the rounded edges straight. Glue 2 together horizontally; do the same with the other 2.

9. Before adding the roof slabs, fill the house with a selection of sweets of your choice.

10. Glue each roof carefully to each side of the 45° angled edges. Wait until completely dry. You may need to hold the roof in place until the chocolate has dried.

11. Glue the milk chocolate Wonder bars in place on either side of the front and back of the house (see the photo).

12. For the doors, use the remaining 2 slabs of ebony and ivory chocolate to cut out two 2 × 3 doors and four 2 × 2 windows (see the photo). Glue them firmly in place with melted chocolate.

13. Using any remaining melted chocolate (or melt more if needed), decorate your house with sweets of your choice.

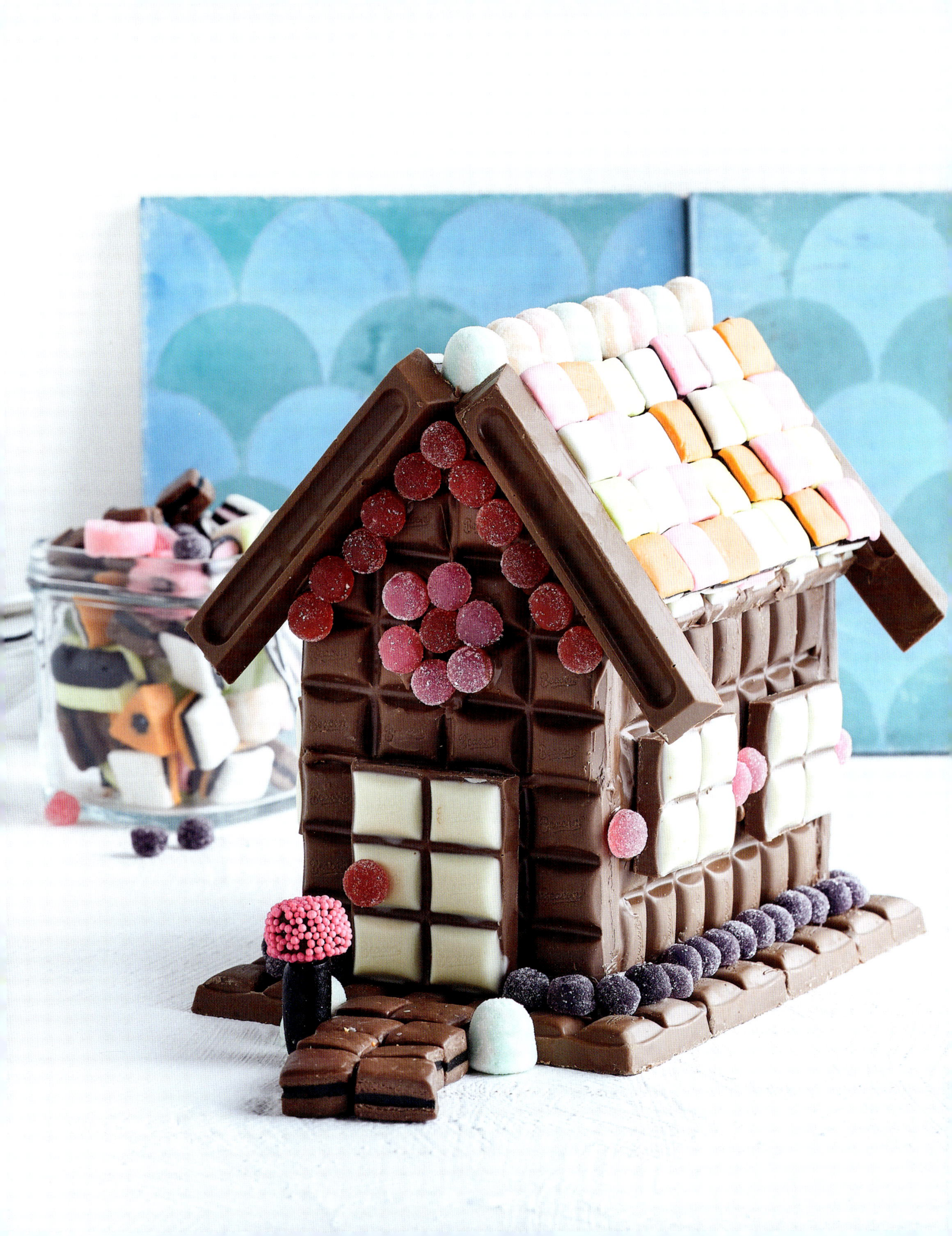

Chilli Choc
SPICE CREAM POPS

The perfect balance of sweet and spicy and they're sooo simple to make!

Grated rind of 1 orange
5 ml Robertsons chilli flakes
45 ml fresh cream
2-litre tub Ola Rich 'n Creamy chocolate ice cream
Dark chocolate slab for coating

1. Mix the orange rind and chilli flakes with the cream and heat for 1 minute on the stove top.

2. Soften the ice cream in the fridge for 1–2 hours until you can stir it. Then add the infused cream. Mix well.

3. Spoon into moulds, insert an ice cream stick and freeze.

4. Remove from the freezer and drizzle each pop with melted chocolate.

5. Sprinkle with chilli flakes and orange zest and serve on a bed of crushed ice.

Cinnamon and Ginger Spice CREAM POPS

Fuss-free dessert pops with a crunchy cookie crust and a kick of spice.

12–15 crushed ginger cookies
7,5 ml Robertsons ground ginger
10 ml Robertsons ground cinnamon
45 ml fresh cream
2-litre tub Ola Rich 'n Creamy vanilla ice cream
Cupcake liners

1. Position cupcake liners in the cups of a 12-cup muffin tin.

2. Crush the ginger cookies in a food processor and place some dust in the base of each cupcake liner.

3. Mix the ground ginger and cinnamon with the fresh cream and heat for 1 minute on the stove.

4. Soften the ice cream in the fridge for 1–2 hours until you can stir it. Then add the infused cream. Mix well and spoon into the cupcake liners in the muffin tin.

5. Insert an ice cream stick, sprinkle with more crushed biscuits and pop into the freezer to set.

6. Remove the pops from the mould and remove the cupcake liners before serving.

Dit lyk maklik en na iets anders!
– SANDRA BRITS

Christmas Cake

A super simple chocolate Christmas cake made using a pack of muffin mix!

FOR THE CAKE
4 eggs
1 ⅗ cups milk
1 ⅗ cups oil
1 kg (or 2 × 500 g packets) Sasko chocolate muffin mix
1 tsp ground cinnamon
½ tsp ground nutmeg
200 g Safari pecan nuts
200 g Moir's glacé cherries
500 g Safari sun-dried cake mix

FOR THE ICING
3 egg whites
500 g icing sugar
50 g sweetened cocoa powder

1. Preheat the oven to 160 °C.

2. Mix the eggs with the milk and oil in a bowl.

3. In a separate bowl, mix the chocolate muffin mix with the ground cinnamon and nutmeg.

4. Pour in the liquid mixture and combine with a hand-held mixer until smooth.

5. Roughly chop the pecan nuts and cherries.

6. Fold the nuts, cherries and cake mix into the cake batter.

7. Pour the cake batter into a greased 25 cm cake tin and bake for 60–90 minutes in the preheated oven.

8. For the icing, combine the egg whites in a bowl with the icing sugar. Be sure to use a sieve for the icing sugar to avoid lumps. Mix until smooth.

9. Once the cake has completely cooled, spread the icing over the cake and place it in the fridge for 10–15 minutes to set.

10. Place a stencil over the iced cake. Spoon the sweetened cocoa into a sieve and shake over the stencil until it is completely covered. Slice and serve.

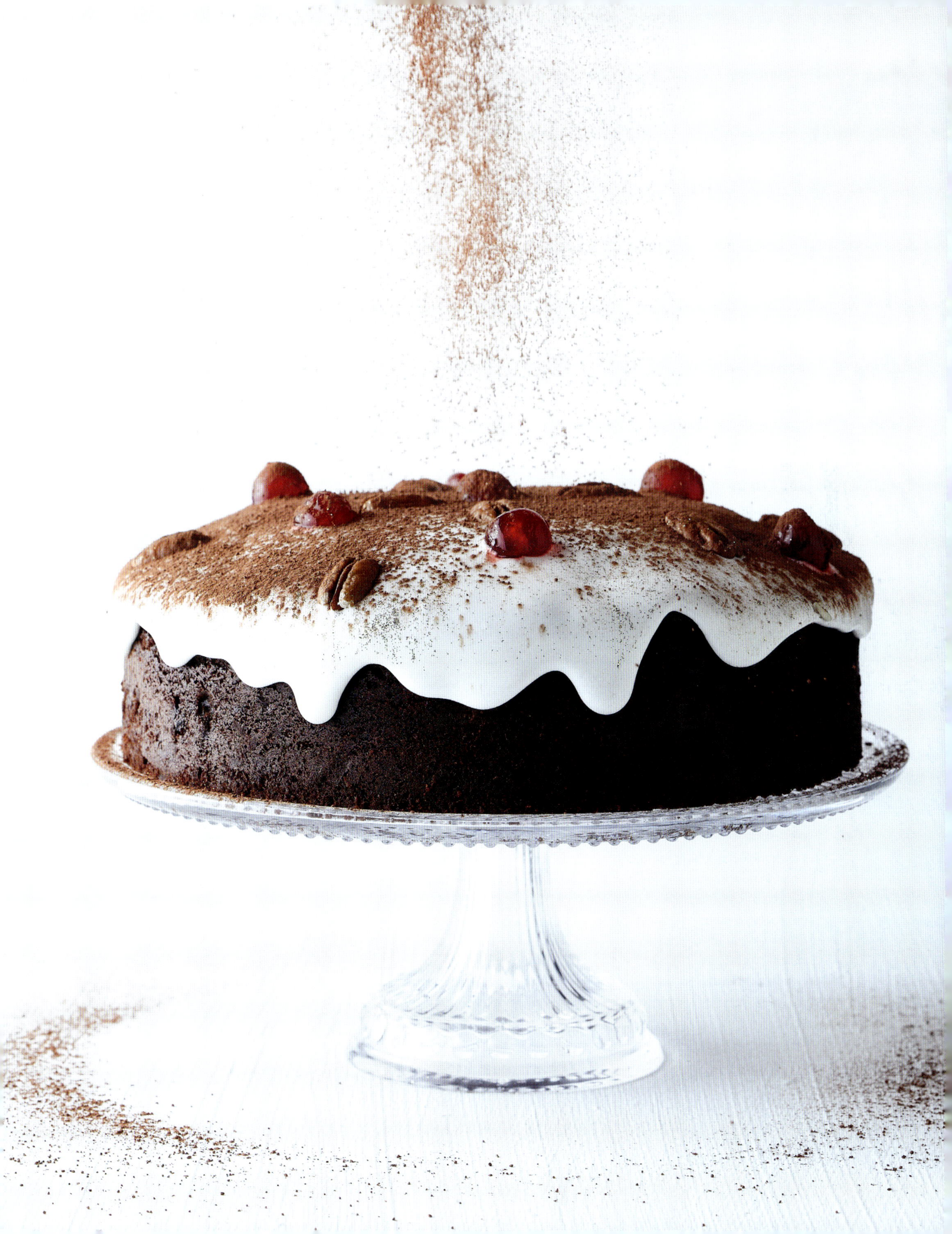

Christmas ICE CREAM CAKE

CAKE LAYER
500 g Food Lover's Market luxury festive cake mix
½ cup sherry, brandy, rum or brewed tea, plus extra for feeding
Zest and juice of 2 oranges and 1 lemon
125 g unsalted butter, softened
125 g light brown sugar
1 tsp vanilla essence
2 eggs
100 g flour
1 tsp ground mixed spice
50 g whole or flaked nuts of your choice (optional)

ICE CREAM LAYER
2 cups Food Lover's Market luxury festive cake mix
Sherry, brandy, rum or tea for soaking
4 cups vanilla ice cream

TOPPINGS
½ slab milk chocolate, melted
½ can caramel treat, melted
1 cup crushed chocolate
Food Lover's Market Nuggles (chocolate coated nuts or raisins), optional
½ cup pecan nuts

1. Place the luxury festive cake mix into a bowl with your choice of alcohol or tea, citrus zest and juice. Mix well. Cover and leave to soak overnight.

2. Preheat the oven to 160 °C. Butter and double-line a 23–25 cm diameter cake tin with baking paper.

3. Beat the butter, sugar and vanilla essence until creamy. Then beat in the eggs one by one.

4. Tip in the flour, mixed spice, soaked dried fruit and any liquid from the bowl, plus your chosen nuts, and stir. Scrape the mixture into the cake tin. Using the back of your spoon, make a slight dent in the centre of the mixture. Then bake for 1 hour in the preheated oven.

5. Reduce the oven temperature to 140 °C, loosely cover the top of the cake with a double sheet of foil or baking parchment, and bake for 30 minutes or until a skewer poked to the bottom comes out clean.

6. Cool in the tin, then lift out and wrap in baking paper.

7. For the ice cream layer, soak the cake mix overnight in enough rum/sherry/brandy/tea/juice to cover the cake mix completely.

8. Let the ice cream soften slightly before mixing in the soaked cake mix.

9. Line the same-sized cake tin with plastic wrap before pressing the ice cream into then. Pop into the freezer for at least an hour.

10. To assemble the cake, ensure that the cake layer is completely cooled. Place on a plate and top with the ice cream layer.

11. Drizzle with melted chocolate and caramel and sprinkle with crushed chocolate, pecan nuts and Nuggles, if using. Serve immediately.

CHRISTMAS CAKE
Crumpet Stack

Light and fluffy crumpets + layers of melted chocolate + berries + cream = the simplest, most stunning Christmas cake EVER!

1½ tbsp Stork margarine, melted
2 eggs
5 tbsp white granulated sugar
2 cups milk
2 cups cake flour
5 tbsp unsweetened cocoa powder
4 tsp baking powder
⅓ tsp salt
½ cup Christmas fruit mix, finely chopped
225 g Stork margarine
1½ cups chocolate, broken into pieces
Extra margarine for cooking the crumpets
1 cup cream, whipped until fluffy
1 punnet of strawberries, sliced
Icing sugar

> We grew so enthusiastic that we traipsed to a berry farm for fresh pickings: our version is going to be white with white chocolate to match our Christmas/family day theme. Awesome idea!
> **– KARIN PANAINO PETERSEN**

1. Melt 1½ tablespoons of margarine in a saucepan.

2. Add the eggs to a mixing bowl and whisk while gradually adding the sugar.

3. Add the milk and the melted margarine to the egg mixture. Stir well.

4. Sift the flour, cocoa powder, baking powder and salt and add to the egg mixture.

5. Add the Christmas fruit mix and stir to combine.

6. To make a chocolate ganache, heat 225 g Stork margarine in a saucepan until it melts. Once melted, pour it over the chocolate pieces and stir continuously until it is melted and velvety. Let it cool to thicken.

7. Heat margarine in a small or medium-sized frying pan. Spoon the batter into the pan so that it is completely covered and cook until the bottom is browned. Flip the crumpet and cook through.

8. Continue with all the crumpet batter until you have 5 large crumpets.

9. Once cooled, spread a layer of ganache to the edges of the crumpet. Cover with a thicker layer of whipped cream. Add a single layer of sliced strawberries, pressing them gently into the whipped cream. Repeat with the remaining crumpet layers.

10. For the top layer, spread the remaining chocolate ganache over the top crumpet followed by whipped cream and fresh berries to garnish.

11. Sift a dusting of icing sugar over the stack before serving.

Steri Stumpie HOT CHOCOLATE

You HAVE to taste this to believe how delicious it is!

80 g milk chocolate
1 cup Paramalat fresh cream
2 × 350 ml bottles of chocolate Steri Stumpie
About 2 handfuls mini marshmallows
1–2 tbsp unsweetened cocoa powder

1. Melt the milk chocolate in a bowl over hot water.
2. Once melted, drizzle the chocolate into 4 ovenproof mugs.
3. Preheat the oven to 180 °C.
4. Divide the cream and Steri Stumpie among the 4 mugs.
5. Top with mini marshmallows.
6. Place the mugs in the oven for 5–8 minutes or until the marshmallows are toasted.
7. Drizzle the remaining melted chocolate over the marshmallows.
8. Top each mug with a generous dusting of sifted cocoa powder.
9. Serve with your favourite biscuits for dipping.

Unreal!

No-bake LAYERED CHEESECAKE

Wow! This beautiful cheesecake is an excellent make-ahead dessert option for summer!

FOR THE BISCUIT BASE
250 g vanilla biscuits
50 g butter, melted

FOR THE CHEESECAKE
200 g strawberries
2 cups Liqui-Fruit cranberry kiwi twist
200 g blueberries
500 g cream cheese
1 cup icing sugar
1 ⅓ cup thick cream

FOR THE TOPPING
Kiwis, strawberries and blueberries, to garnish

1. Grease and line the base and side of a springform cake tin with baking paper.

2. Place the biscuits and melted butter in a food processor and process until finely crushed. Spoon the mixture evenly over the base of the prepared pan. Press down and place in the freezer to set.

3. Meanwhile, place the strawberries in a small saucepan over low heat together with 1 cup cranberry kiwi twist fruit juice. Cook, stirring, and using the back of the spoon to gently crush the berries, for approximately 10 minutes or until the strawberries break down and a syrupy consistency is achieved. Remove from the heat.

4. Use a fork to mash the strawberries before straining the mixture through a fine sieve into a bowl, using the back of a spoon to push through as much pulp as possible. Set aside.

5. Repeat the process with the blueberries and the remaining cup of cranberry kiwi twist fruit juice.

6. Place the cream cheese and icing sugar in a food processor and process until smooth. Add the thick cream and blitz once more until smooth.

7. Divide the cream cheese mixture evenly among two bowls. Add the strawberry purée to the first bowl and the blueberry purée to the second, stir to combine.

8. Pour the strawberry mixture into the base of the prepared pan.

9. Refrigerate for 2 hours or until firm.

10. Pour the blueberry mixture evenly over the set strawberry mixture.

11. Refrigerate for 4 hours.

12. Remove the cheesecake from the springform pan and place on a serving plate. Top the cheesecake with kiwis, strawberries and blueberries before serving.

Amarula
CHOCOLATE CRÊPE PARCELS

A scoop of vanilla ice cream, smothered in a sticky Amarula sauce, wrapped in a chocolate crêpe ... Amarula lovers, be warned!

FOR THE CRÊPES
1 cup all-purpose flour
½ cup Amarula
1½ cups milk
2 eggs
2 tbsp granulated sugar
1 tsp vanilla essence
2 tbsp unsweetened cocoa powder
Oil for frying
Vanilla ice cream
Nuts (optional)
Honeycomb, to garnish

FOR THE AMARULA COCONUT CARAMEL SAUCE
¾ cup unsalted butter
1½ cups brown sugar
2 tbsps water
¼ tsp salt
1 tbsp honey
¼ cup coconut milk
¼ cup Amarula cream liqueur

1. In a mixing bowl, combine the flour, Amarula, milk, eggs, sugar, vanilla essence and cocoa powder.

2. Heat a lightly greased skillet or pancake pan.

3. Remove the skillet from the heat and add 2 tablespoons of batter.

4. Lift and tilt to spread the batter around the pan.

5. Return the pan to the heat and brown the crêpe on one side.

6. Repeat until all the crêpes are cooked. Once cooked, set aside.

7. Add the butter, brown sugar, water and salt to a medium-sized saucepan and heat over medium heat, stirring until the butter melts.

8. Bring to the boil for 5 minutes, stirring occasionally.

9. Reduce the heat and stir in the honey, coconut milk and Amarula. The caramel will continue to thicken upon stirring and standing.

10. To assemble the crêpe parcels, add a scoop of ice cream to the centre of each crêpe, as well as a tablespoon of the coconut caramel sauce and a sprinkling of nuts.

11. Raise the crêpe edges, bring together and tie with a small piece of twine to make a parcel (discard the twine before eating). Garnish with honeycomb pieces.

12. Serve and slice open to reveal the indulgent centre.

Drinks

Deep Purple G&T

A mind-blowing basil and beetroot infusion that tastes delicious and looks AMAZING!

3 beetroots, well washed
1 cup Bombay Sapphire gin
Fresh basil leaves
Cucumber slices, to garnish
Schweppes tonic water, to serve

1. With a potato peeler, finely slice the beetroot.

2. In an airtight container, refrigerate the gin together with the beetroot slices overnight to allow the beetroot to dye the gin a deep purple.

3. Strain the gin before serving.

4. Finely chop some fresh basil leaves. Fill a jug with water and add the chopped basil leaves, allowing these to infuse in the water. Place in the fridge for 1 hour.

5. Strain out the leaves, leaving only the clear infused water.

6. Place a basil leaf into each hole of an ice cube tray, cover with infused water and freeze.

7. Serve your cocktail with 2 basil-infused ice blocks, 2 shots of beetroot-infused gin, cucumber slices and Schweppes tonic water.

DRINKS | 191

BLUEBERRY-INFUSED G&T
with
MINT AND LIME SORBET

A good old G&T + a bold burst of blueberry + a zesty mint and lime sorbet = an awesome drink for hot summer days by the pool ...

FOR THE BLUEBERRY-INFUSED G&T
1 cup blueberries
6 shots Tanqueray No. Ten gin

FOR THE MINT AND LIME SORBET
1 cup water
½ cup honey
½ cup granulated sugar
½ cup fresh mint leaves
1 cup fresh lime juice
1 tsp grated lime zest

TO SERVE
125 ml Schweppes tonic water
Lime slices
Mint leaves

1. Place the blueberries in a jar and muddle them. Cover the crushed blueberries with the gin and refrigerate overnight.

2. In a small saucepan on medium heat, combine 1 cup of water with the honey and sugar.

3. Cook, stirring, until the sugar is completely dissolved, about 2 minutes.

4. Remove the pan from the heat and add the mint leaves. Stir, cover, and let sit for about 15 minutes to bring out the flavours of the mint.

5. Strain the syrup, discarding the mint leaves.

6. Stir in the lime juice and zest. Pour the mixture into a dish. Cover and freeze overnight.

7. Strain the blueberry gin mixture and set the gin aside.

8. To serve, pour a shot of the gin into a glass, top with the Schweppes tonic water and add a scoop of lime and mint sorbet.

9. Serve with lime slices and mint leaves.

> Wow, this looks amaze!
> **– VANETIA MENTOR**

Botanical Bomb G&T

Light, refreshing and bursting with flavour! This might just be our fav G&T recipe of all THYME!

2 sprigs rosemary
2 sprigs thyme
2 sprigs mint
½ tsp coriander seeds
6 shots of Tanqueray No. Ten gin
1 lemon
1 cup ice cubes
Schweppes tonic water, to serve
Rosemary sprigs, to garnish

NOTE: The infusion makes 6 tots. If not using it all at once, keep the infused gin in the fridge to use as needed.

1. Gently bruise the sprigs of rosemary, thyme, mint and coriander seeds in a pestle and mortar before placing into a mason jar.

2. Pour the gin into the mason jar with the bruised herbs and spices.

3. Allow the gin to sit in a fridge for at least 3 hours to infuse.

4. Cut the lemon into quarters and place them cut side down on a hot griddle pan.

5. Once one side of the lemon is charred, turn to char the other side.

6. Strain the gin and set aside.

7. Add the ice cubes to a glass, pour a tot of the infused gin over the ice and top with Schweppes tonic water.

8. Squeeze some of the charred lemon juice into the glass before dropping the lemon in for extra flavour.

9. Garnish with a sprig of rosemary.

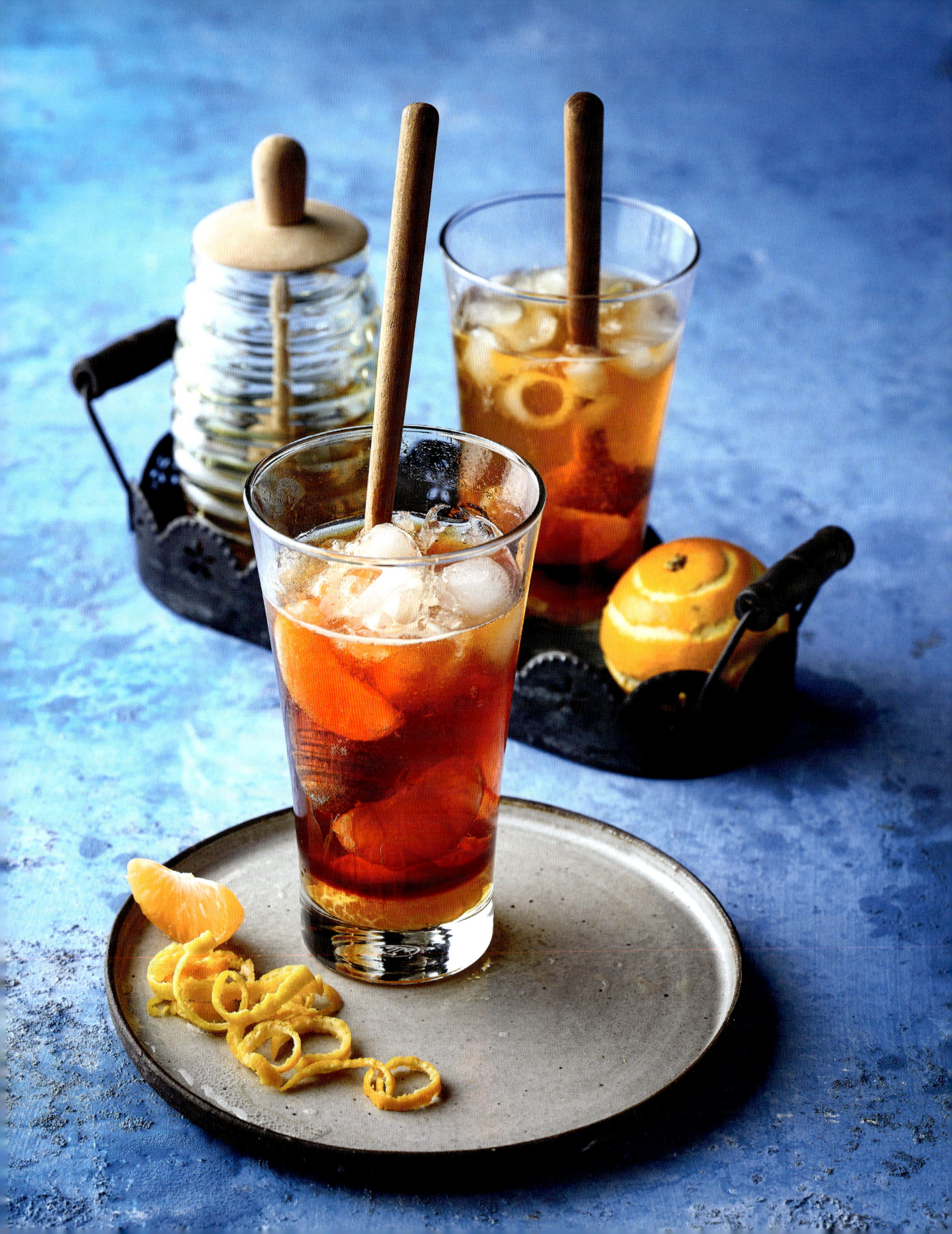

Rooibos and Honey G&Ts

A proudly South African drink featuring honey, rooibos and muddled naartjie segments ... This drink is the perfect marriage of some of our most brilliant local flavours!

12 tbsp Bombay Sapphire gin
2 teabags or 2 tbsp dried rooibos tea leaves
Honey, to taste
Naartjies
Ice cubes
1 × 200 ml can Schweppes tonic water per serving
Fresh mint leaves, to garnish

1. Pour the gin into a teapot with a removable infuser.
2. Add rooibos tea leaves to the infuser and place in the teapot.
3. Add honey to the tea leaves and allow the gin to infuse for 4–6 hours.
4. In a glass jar, muddle a handful of naartjie segments.
5. Grate naartjie zest and set aside.
6. Use a honey spoon to drip honey into 6 glasses for serving.
7. Spoon 1 tablespoon of muddled naartjie pieces into each glass. Top the naartjie pieces with ice cubes.
8. Remove the tea-leaf infuser from the teapot.
9. Pour 1 shot of the infused gin over the muddled naartjies and ice and top with tonic water.
10. Garnish with naartjie zest and fresh mint leaves before serving.

NOTE: If you are not using all the gin infusion at once, keep the remainder in the fridge to use as needed.

ROOIBOS AND GRANADILLA
Punch

A super refreshing rooibos mocktail with the COOLEST ice blocks!

Fresh mint leaves
Fresh berries
Edible flowers
1⅕ cup boiling water
2 rooibos teabags
4 × 330 ml cans Rose's passion fruit and soda flavoured drinks
6 granadillas

NON-ALCOHOLIC

1. Add a selection of mint leaves, berries and edible flowers to two ice trays and cover with water. Freeze overnight.

2. Pour boiling water into a large glass punch bowl and add the rooibos teabags. Allow the tea to strengthen and cool slightly.

3. Pour the passion fruit and soda flavoured drinks into the punch bowl.

4. Drop in the pulp of 3 granadillas. Wash and halve the remaining granadillas and add them to the bowl.

5. Add a few of the prepared ice cubes to each serving glass and pour the punch over to serve.

Honey and Cinnamon-infused PUNCH

Fresh, fruity and fabulous! Gin lovers – this one is for you.

2 peaches, sliced
2 apples, sliced
3 limes, sliced
6 cinnamon sticks
6 tbsp honey
1 cup fresh lime juice
1½ cups Tanqueray No. Ten gin
Ice cubes
Schweppes tonic water
Handful fresh thyme sprigs, to garnish
Cinnamon stick, to garnish

1. Place the slices of peach, apple and lime in a large jug and top with the cinnamon sticks, honey and lime juice.
2. Pour the gin into the jug.
3. Allow the gin to infuse in the fridge overnight.
4. Stir the infused gin before preparing the serving glasses.
5. Place ice cubes in each glass, topped with slices of peach, apple and lime.
6. Pour over the infused gin and top with tonic water.
7. Garnish with a sprig of thyme and a cinnamon stick.

NOTE: This punch will make 15 single-tot servings. If you're not using it all at once, keep the infusion in the fridge until needed. Top each glass with tonic water before serving.

Strawberry VODKA AND LIME POPSICLES

Ice pops are an AWESOME summer treat; alcohol infused pops? Even BETTER!

1 punnet of strawberries
2 tbsp Rose's lemon cordial
2 tbsp water
Sugar to rim the glasses
3 or 4 strawberries per glass, diced
1 shot of vodka per serving
1 × 330 ml can Rose's lime and lemonade flavoured drink per serving
Fresh lime slices, to garnish

Fun factor
10

1. Cut about 5 or 6 of the strawberries into thin slices and set aside.

2. Chop the remaining strawberries into halves and blend them with the lemon cordial and water until you have a purée. Place the sliced strawberries in the popsicle moulds.

3. Pour the strawberry purée into the popsicles moulds, cover and insert the popsicle sticks.

4. Keep some of the purée aside to rim the glasses for serving.

5. Place the popsicles in the freezer for about 3–4 hours or until fully frozen.

6. Rim glass with the remaining strawberry purée and sugar.

7. Add chopped strawberries to the bottom of each glass.

8. Add one shot of vodka to each glass.

9. Place a popsicle stick-side up into each glass.

10. Pour the lime and lemonade flavoured drink into each glass. Then garnish with a lime slice and serve.

So cool!

FRUITY PUNCH SALAD *Mocktail*

NON-ALCOHOLIC

Refreshing and slightly sweet with lots of fizz – this is sure to be the most popular drink at your next party!

Honeydew melon
Watermelon
Cantaloupe (spanspek)
Gooseberries
Grapes
Mint leaves
1 × 330 ml can Rose's lime and lemonade flavoured drink per serving

1. Using a melon baller, remove balls of the melon flesh and set aside.
2. Repeat with the watermelon (leave some slices for step 6) and cantaloupe.
3. Place all the melon balls onto a tray lined with baking paper.
4. Spread the balls out evenly and freeze until set.
5. Once frozen, place the balls into a resealable bag for storage in the freezer.
6. Using cookie cutters, cut star shapes out of the remaining watermelon slices.
7. Place these star shapes onto a skewer stick along with gooseberries and grapes at the ends.
8. Place the skewers into the freezer.
9. Add the frozen melon balls to a tall glass with fresh mint leaves.
10. Top with the lime and lemonade flavoured drink.
11. Serve with the frozen fruity skewers.

LEMON SORBET
Soda Floats

Part fizzy ice cold soda, part light and silky sorbet – these creative mocktails are guaranteed to wow!

NON-ALCOHOLIC

2 cups water
1 cup sugar
¾ cup Rose's lemon cordial
Lemon zest
Freshly squeezed juice of 1 lemon
1 × 330 ml can Rose's dry lemon drink
Raspberries
1 × 330 ml Rose's passion fruit and lemonade flavoured drink
Granadilla pulp
1 × 330 ml Rose's lime and lemonade flavoured drink
Lime wedges
Mint leaves

1. Bring the water to the boil with the sugar for 5 minutes.

2. Pour the mixture into a mixing bowl together with the lemon cordial, lemon zest and juice. Stir to combine.

3. Freeze the mixture for 4–6 hours.

4. Using an egg beater, beat the mixture until smooth and place back in the freezer for another 4–6 hours.

5. Repeat the beating and freezing process twice more.

6. Once ready, scoop out balls of the sorbet and place 2 balls in each glass.

7. In the first glass, serve the lemon sorbet with the dry lemon drink and fresh raspberries.

8. In the second glass, serve the sorbet balls with the passion fruit and lemonade drink, topped with granadilla pulp.

9. In the third glass, serve the sorbet balls with the lime and lemonade drink and lime wedges.

10. Garnish the glasses with fresh mint leaves.

DRINKS | 201

COCONUT AND LIME
Slushie

NON-ALCOHOLIC

A creamy cocktail that's so freakin' nice. Add a splash of rum, or don't – either way, this cocktail has P-A-R-T-Y written all over it!

½–¾ cup coconut flakes
5 cups ice cubes
3 tbsp Rose's lime cordial
1 cup coconut cream
Fresh lime slices, to garnish

1. Toast the coconut flakes in a pan over a medium heat until golden and set aside.

2. Add the ice cubes, lime cordial and coconut cream to a blender and blend until smooth.

3. Rim the chilled serving glasses with toasted coconut flakes.

4. Pipe or spoon the mixture into tall glasses.

5. Garnish with fresh lime slices and a sprinkling of toasted coconut flakes.

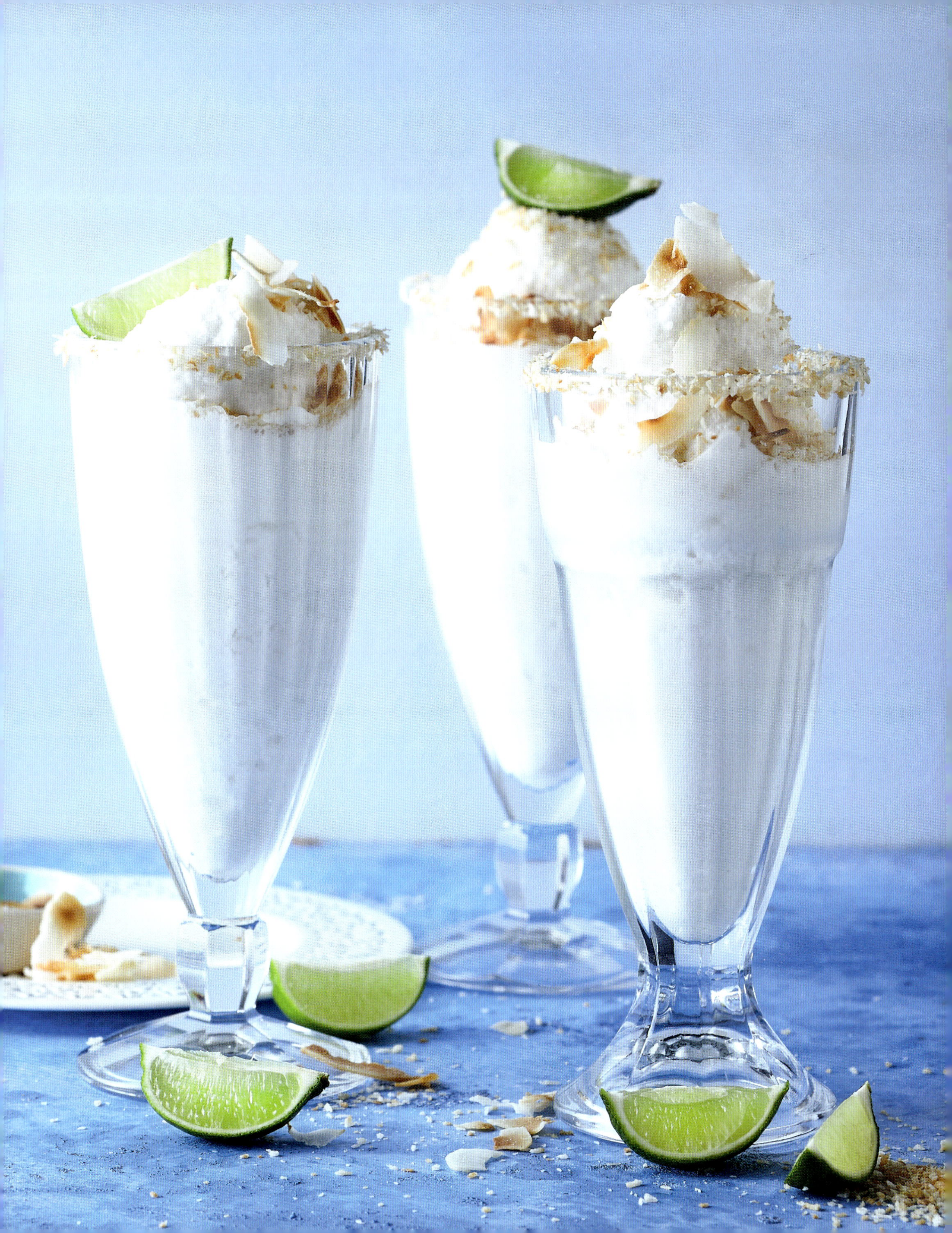

STRAWBERRY STINGER
Slushie

Serve this drink on practically any occasion ...

1 cup sugar
1 cup water
1 punnet strawberries
Lemons, sufficient for 1⅕ cup juice
2 cups litchi juice
2 shots Grey Goose vodka
1 × 200 ml can Schweppes lemonade per serving
Mint leaves

1. In a medium-sized pan, bring the sugar, water and strawberries to the boil. Simmer until a syrupy consistency is achieved.

2. Strain, pour into a jug and set aside.

3. Juice the lemons for roughly 1⅕ cups juice and pour into an ice cube tray.

4. Pour the litchi juice into a second ice cube tray.

5. Pour strawberry syrup into a third ice cube tray.

6. Place the ice cube trays in the freezer until set.

7. Label resealable bags for storing each ice cube flavour separately. Place the ice cubes in their respective bags and keep frozen.

8. Heat the remaining strawberry syrup over low heat so that it can thicken further into a reduction.

9. Place 7 strawberry ice cubes, 5 litchi ice cubes and 3 lemon ice cubes into a blender with a splash of litchi juice and 2 shots of vodka. Blend until smooth.

10. Pour the mixture into tall glasses, topping with the strawberry reduction and lemonade.

11. Stir, garnish with fresh mint leaves and serve.

Watermelon and Lime SLUSHIE

NON-ALCOHOLIC

Only a handful of ingredients ... and it's sooo tasty!

1 watermelon
½ cup Rose's lime cordial
1 tbsp honey
Mint leaves
1 lime

NOTE: This is a giant slushie served in a watermelon with loads of straws! If you prefer, use a ladle to scoop out individual servings.

1. Slice the watermelon in half. Use a melon baller to remove balls of watermelon (and create a watermelon 'bowl' in the process).

2. Place the watermelon balls into a resealable bag and freeze for 3 hours.

3. Add the frozen melon balls to a blender along with the lime cordial.

4. Add the honey and the mint leaves to the blender.

5. Blend until smooth.

6. Pour the slushie mixture into the watermelon 'bowl'.

7. Squeeze fresh lime juice over the slushie and serve immediately.

8. Garnish with twisted lime slices, straws and umbrellas.

206 | DRINKS

POMEGRANATE SORBET
Mojito

A drink with a difference – this mojito contains pomegranate seeds and a scoop of zesty lime and mint sorbet!

1 cup water
1 cup sugar
Fresh mint leaves
3 limes
½ cup sugar
Ice cubes
1 shot Bacardi rum per serving
Pomegranate seeds
1 × 200 ml can Schweppes soda water per serving

1. In a small saucepan, bring the water, sugar and fresh mint leaves to the boil. Allow to simmer until the mint has infused.

2. Strain the mixture and set aside. Grate lime zest and set aside, juice the limes into a bowl and add the juice to the strained mint syrup. Stir in the lime zest.

3. Finely chop the mint leaves, add to the mixture and stir. Pour into a bowl and freeze the sorbet mixture overnight.

4. In a cocktail shaker, muddle fresh mint leaves with sugar, top with ice cubes and pour in 1 shot of rum and shake.

5. Add the pomegranate seeds to the glass before adding a scoop of sorbet.

6. Pour the cocktail mixture over the sorbet, top with soda water and serve.

AMARULA *Coco*

Two deliciously creamy cocktail ideas featuring your favourite African liqueur!

AMARULA COCO MARTINI
2 cups Amarula cream liqueur
2 cups coconut water
1 tsp honey
1 tbsp toasted coconut bits
1½ cup crushed ice
1 coconut ribbon

AMARULA COCO SLUSHIE
½ cup coconut cream
1 tbsp honey
1 vanilla pod
A few blocks of ice (enough to achieve a slushie consistency)
1 coconut, cut in half for serving
Dark chocolate shards
Fresh mint leaves

COCO MARTINI

1. In a cocktail shaker, mix the Amarula with the coconut water and shake.

2. Rim 2 glasses with the honey and toasted coconut bits.

3. Pour half of the mixture over ice in a chilled martini glass. (Set the other half aside.)

4. Serve with a coconut ribbon woven through the ice.

COCO SLUSHIE

1. Put the other half of the cocktail mix from the coco martini into a blender with the coconut cream, honey, the seeds of the vanilla pod and ice.

2. Blend until smooth.

3. Pour the icy mixture into two coconut halves. Top with shards of dark chocolate, fresh mint leaves and a paper straw and serve.

Spiced Amarula
ROOIBOS LATTE

An irresistibly smooth hot drink – best enjoyed curled up near a cozy fire or in bed with a good book!

3 tbsp loose leaf rooibos tea
5 crushed cardamon pods
½ tsp allspice
1 cinnamon stick
5 whole cloves
Thumb-size piece of ginger cut into rounds
1 star anise
2 cups boiling water
¼ cup cream
½ cup Amarula cream liqueur
Enough milk for 3 cups, frothed
¼ tsp ground cinnamon for garnishing
1 whole star anise for garnishing
Honey, to drizzle

1. Place the tea leaves and all the spices in the tea strainer.
2. Fill the teapot with boiling water and place the strainer inside.
3. Allow to steep for 15 minutes.
4. Pour the steeped tea into a small saucepan through a strainer and discard the spices.
5. Pour the cream into the spiced rooibos tea and add the Amarula.
6. Bring the mixture to an almost boil and then remove from the heat, stirring continuously.
7. Pour the latte into a transparent heat-resistant glasses and top with frothed milk, a dusting of cinnamon and 1 whole star anise.
8. Top with a generous drizzle of honey (using a honey spoon) and serve.

DRINKS | 209

COFFEE-INFUSED
Vodka Soda

A quenching cocktail made with home-made coffee-infused vodka. Delish!

¾ cup coffee beans
9 shots Cîroc vodka
80 g slab milk chocolate
Honey
Crushed ice
1 × 200 ml can Schweppes lemonade
1 × 200 ml can Schweppes soda water

1. Place ½ cup of the coffee beans into a large jar and top with the vodka.
2. Place in the fridge and let it infuse overnight.
3. Melt the chocolate. Drizzle the melted chocolate over ¼ cup roasted coffee beans and allow to set.
4. Remove the infused vodka from the fridge and strain.
5. Drizzle honey along the inside of chilled tall glasses and add crushed ice to the glass.
6. Pour lemonade and soda water into each glass.
7. Pour the infused vodka slowly into the glass to create layers.
8. Garnish with the chocolate-covered coffee beans serve.

> Now this is talking loudly to me!
> – **PETRUS SMIT**

Refreshing!

Festive HOLIDAY SANGRIA

A deliciously refreshing drink ... great for lazy days when you're just lounging around!

3 oranges
3 pears
Seeds of 1 pomegranate
3 cups white wine
⅗ cup ginger beer
½ cup brandy
1⅖ cups Liqui-Fruit sparkling apple juice plus extra for serving
Cinnamon sugar for the rims of glasses (optional)
Ice cubes
3 cinnamon sticks

1. Slice the oranges and pears.

2. Remove the pomegranate seeds into a bowl.

3. In a large pitcher or punch bowl, combine the white wine, ginger beer, brandy and sparkling apple juice.

4. Add the sliced fruit to the pitcher.

5. Stir and then refrigerate until chilled.

6. Before serving, rim your glasses with cinnamon sugar. Fill each glass with ice and pour the sangria over the ice. NOTE: This recipe will make enough for 6–8 glasses.

7. Top with an extra splash of sparkling apple juice.

8. Garnish with slices of pears, oranges, pomegranate seeds and a cinnamon stick.

9. Drink up!

WHISKY
Peach Iced Tea

Perfect for parties – get a few friends together this weekend so you can try it!

7 rooibos teabags
8 cups boiling water
5 peaches
2 handfuls strawberries
1½ cups sugar
2 cups water
6 shots Three Ships Bourbon Cask whisky
2 × 200 ml cans Schweppes lemonade
2 × 200 ml cans Schweppes soda water
1–2 lemons
Ice cubes
Mint leaves

1. Place the rooibos teabags in a large heatproof glass dispenser and top with the boiling water. Allow to strengthen for 5 minutes before removing the teabags.

2. Slice 3 of the peaches and 1 handful of the strawberries.

3. Place the fruit in a medium-sized pan with the sugar and water.

4. Bring to a boil and simmer for 20–30 minutes.

5. Strain the syrup and pour into the glass dispenser with the tea. Discard the fruit.

6. Add 6 shots of whisky, the lemonade and the soda water to the glass dispenser.

7. Slice the lemons, remaining 2 peaches and the other handful of strawberries. Place these together with ice cubes into the glass dispenser.

8. Prepare the glasses by filling them with ice cubes and fruit slices from the glass dispenser.

9. Pour the iced tea mixture over the ice cubes and serve.

Mixed Berry SANGRIA

From a book club to a braai – this drink will get any party started!

2 punnets strawberries
2 cups blueberries
1 cup blackberries
1 cup vodka
2–3 apples
Handful mint leaves
1½ cups sugar
2 cups water
2 cups 4th Street sweet red wine
Ice cubes
2 × 200 ml cans Schweppes ginger ale
2 × 200 ml cans Schweppes soda water
Extra sugar for rimming the glasses (optional)

1. Roughly chop half of the strawberries, blueberries and blackberries. Add the berries to a glass bowl and top with the vodka. Refrigerate overnight.

2. Chop the remaining blackberries, blueberries and strawberries, as well as the apples and mint leaves.

3. Place the chopped fruit and mint in a large pot or pan with the sugar and water.

4. Bring to a boil and simmer until a syrupy consistency is achieved. Strain and set aside to cool.

5. Pour the vodka-soaked berries into a large glass dispenser, followed by the syrup. Reserve ¼ cup of the syrup for serving.

6. Add the sweet red wine, ice cubes, ginger ale and soda water.

7. Rim the serving glasses (6–8 or more) by dipping them into the reserved syrup and then in sugar before pouring sangria into the glasses to serve.

Berrylicious!

BERRY ROSÉ *Spritzer*

Rosé + fresh berries + soda water + lots of ice = a summer drink you'll really enjoy!

1 cup strawberries, halved
1 cup sugar
1 cup water
2 cups ice
125 g raspberries
180 g blueberries
2 cups 4th Street sweet rosé
1 cup soda water
Fresh mint leaves, to serve

1. Place the halved strawberries in a frying pan. Add the sugar and then the water.

2. Bring to the boil and then allow to simmer for 15 minutes or until the liquid has reduced to a syrup-like consistency (remember, the liquid will thicken further once allowed to cool).

3. Strain the strawberry liquid through a sieve and set aside to cool.

4. In a glass jug, place about 2 cups of ice and the raspberries and blueberries.

5. Pour the strawberry syrup into the jug over the ice and berries.

6. Pour in the 4th Street sweet rosé followed by the soda water.

7. Stir the spritzer until well mixed.

8. Serve with a sprig of mint.

Sparkling GRANADILLA BERRY SMASH

Fun and fizzy fresh fruit cocktail – ideal for pool parties, family lunches or spontaneous summer nights!

1 cup blueberries
2 tbsp Rose's passion fruit cordial
1 granadilla, cut in half
Handful of fresh mint leaves
Ice cubes, crushed
½ cup sparkling white wine
½ cup soda

FOR THE GARNISH
Mint leaves
Frozen raspberries
Granadilla pulp
Slices of lemon

1. Place the blueberries into the bottom of 2 glasses (½ cup per glass) and muddle them.

2. Top the muddled berries with the passion fruit cordial and the granadilla pulp.

3. Place the mint leaves over the muddled fruit and top the mint with crushed ice cubes.

4. Top off the 2 glasses by pouring sparkling wine and soda over the crushed ice.

5. Garnish with a sprig of mint, frozen raspberries, granadilla pulp and lemon slices.

RECIPE INDEX

Page numbers in **bold** indicate photographs.

A

Almonds
  Breakfast pizza 40
  Cocoa and mint berrylicious bowl 44
Apples
  Apple flapjacks 158
  Farm-style apple pies 156, **157**
  Honey and cinnamon-infused punch 197
  Mixed berry sangria 214, **215**
Avocado
  Bread pizza 87
  Cocoa and mint berrylicious bowl 44
  Jars on the go 100, **101**
  Roast butternut salad 124, **125**
  Sheet pan fajita feast 114
  Shredded chicken tacos 81
  Stuffed sweet potatoes 122

B

Bacon
  Bacon-wrapped breakfast stack 34, **35**
  Breakfast baguette 37
  Butternut soup 126
  Cheeseburger bites **54**, 55
  Cheesy egg toasty **12–13**, 13
  Creamy bacon alfredo 97
  Double cheese pizza pinwheel 138, **139**
  Hash brown breakfast pizza 18, **18**, **19**
  Mac 'n' cheese burger **92**, 93
  Maize balls in a creamy bacon sauce 91
  Mealie meal muffins **38–39**, 39
  Muffins in mugs 52, **52**
  Pap in a pumpkin 134, **135**
  Spicy lentil and split pea soup 118

Bananas
  Banana and strawberry lava smoothies 44
  Banana fritters with toffee sauce 159
  Cocoa and mint berrylicious bowl 44
  Frozen smoothie cake 146
  Layered chocolate rice pudding 150
  Peanut butter choc power smoothie 42, **43**
  Strawberry smoothie with chia seed pudding 45
Barley
  Chicken and barley bake 80
  Lettuce burgers **116**, 117
Basil
  Caprese pull-apart bread **66**, 67
  Easy Caprese pastry squares 50, **51**
Beans *see also* Green beans
  Bean burgers 123
  Breakfast baguette 37
  Cheesy rice casserole 102, **103**
  Chilli con carne skillet 84, **85**
  Chilli con carne stuffed sweet potatoes 86
  Pap in a pumpkin 134, **135**
  Rice fritter stack **108**, 109
  Sausage and bean spaghetti 96
  Spicy bean dip 70, **71**
  Stuffed peppers 128, **129**
  White bean shakshuka 41
Beef
  Baked spaghetti pie 94, **95**
  Cheeseburger bites **54**, 55
  Chilli con carne skillet 84, **85**
  Chilli con carne stuffed sweet potatoes 86
  Garlic steak foil pack **82**, 83
  Massive mince bun bake 90
  Meatball lasagne soup 76, **76**
  Pasta pie 119

  Ribeye on a cedar plank with a bone marrow cross-section **130**, 131
Beetroot
  Deep purple G&T 190, **191**
  Green spinach and split pea pizza 112, **113**
  Roast butternut salad 124, **125**
Beverages (alcoholic)
  Amarula coco 208
  Berry rosé spritzer 216
  Blueberry-infused G&T with mint and lime sorbet 192
  Botanical bomb G&T 193
  Coffee-infused vodka soda 210, **211**
  Deep purple G&T 190, **191**
  Festive holiday sangria 212
  Honey and cinnamon-infused punch 197
  Mixed berry sangria 214, **215**
  Pomegranate sorbet mojito **206**, 207
  Rooibos and honey G&Ts **194**, 195
  Sparkling granadilla berry smash 217
  Spiced Amarula rooibos latte 209
  Strawberry stinger slushie 204
  Strawberry vodka and lime popsicles 198, **199**
  Whisky peach iced tea 213
Beverages (non-alcoholic)
  Coconut and lime slushie 202, **203**
  Fruity punch salad mocktail 200
  Lemon sorbet soda floats 201
  Rooibos and granadilla punch 196
  Watermelon and lime slushie 205
Biltong
  Biltong and cheese roll-ups 60
  Cheesy maize bites 65
  Cheesy rice snacks 73
  Cream cheese biltong bites 141
  Croque meneer 26, **27**

218 | INDEX

Blackberries
   Mixed berry sangria 214, **215**
Blueberries
   Berry rosé spritzer 216
   Blueberry-infused G&T with mint and lime sorbet 192
   Froyo sarmies 163
   Frozen smoothie cake 146
   Fruit and nut yoghurt bars 46
   Mixed berry sangria 214, **215**
   No-bake layered cheesecake 186
   Rainbow popsicles 168, **169**
   Sheet pan pancakes **24**, 25
   Smoothie swirl popsicles 45
   Sparkling granadilla berry smash 217
Boerewors *see* Sausages
Breads
   Caprese pull-apart bread **66**, 67
   Chakalaka bread 58, **59**
   Cheese and onion potbrood 137
   Cheesy bread boat 61
Breakfast
   Bacon-wrapped breakfast stack 34, **35**
   Banana and strawberry lava smoothies 44
   Bovril French toast roll-ups 36
   Breakfast baguette 37
   Breakfast pizza 40
   Cheesy egg toasty **12–13**, 13
   Croque meneer 26, **27**
   Fruit and nut yoghurt bars 46
   Hash brown breakfast pizza 18, **18**, **19**
   Mealie meal muffins **38–39**, 39
   Peanut butter choc power smoothie 42, **43**
   Sheet pan pancakes **24**, 25
   Smoothies four ways 44, 45
   Super yummy breakfast bars 47
   White bean shakshuka 41
Broccoli
   Chicken and broccoli puff pastry ring 74, **75**
Burgers
   Bean burgers 123
   Cheeseburger bites **54**, 55
   Lettuce burgers **116**, 117
   Mac 'n' cheese burger **92**, 93

Butternut
   Butternut soup 126
   Roast butternut salad 124, **125**
   Stuffed butternut 127
   Vegetable lasagne 115

C

Cabbage
   Cabbage rice roll-ups 106, **107**
   Shredded chicken tacos 81
Cakes *see also* Cheesecakes, Cupcakes
   5-minute mug cake 167
   Christmas cake 180, **181**
   Christmas cake crumpet stack 183
   Christmas ice cream cake 182
   Frozen smoothie cake 146
   Pancake cake **16–17**, 17
Caramel
   Amarula chocolate crêpe parcels 187
   Apple flapjacks 158
   Christmas ice cream cake 182
   Peppermint crisp trifle cups **160**, 161
   S'mores dip 14, **14**, **15**
Cashew nuts
   Marshmallow and popcorn squares 152, **153**
Cheese
   A-maize-zing chakalaka dippers 72
   Bacon-wrapped breakfast stack 34, **35**
   Biltong and cheese roll-ups 60
   Boerie pies 132
   Bovril French toast roll-ups 36
   Bread pizza 87
   Breakfast baguette 37
   Cabbage rice roll-ups 106, **107**
   Calzone dippers 68
   Caprese pull-apart bread **66**, 67
   Cheese and onion potbrood 137
   Cheeseburger bites **54**, 55
   Cheesy baked fritter stack 111
   Cheesy braai bomb 136
   Cheesy bread boat 61
   Cheesy egg toasty **12–13**, 13
   Cheesy maize bites 65
   Cheesy rice casserole 102, **103**
   Cheesy rice snacks 73
   Cheesy sago poppers 62, **63**

Chilli con carne skillet 84, **85**
Chilli con carne stuffed sweet potatoes 86
Cran-Brie bites 57
Creamy bacon alfredo 97
Croque meneer 26, **27**
Double cheese pizza pinwheel 138, **139**
Easy Caprese pastry squares 50, **51**
Giant cheese and bov(roll) 53
Green spinach and split pea pizza 112, **113**
Hash brown breakfast pizza 18, **18**, **19**
Jars on the go 100, **101**
Lettuce burgers **116**, 117
Loaded crustless quiche 77
Mac 'n' cheese boerie bites 56
Mac 'n' cheese burger **92**, 93
Maize balls in a creamy bacon sauce 91
Massive mince bun bake 90
Muffins in mugs 52, **52**
Pap in a pumpkin 134, **135**
Pasta pie 119
Pigs in a blanket 140
Shredded chicken tacos 81
Spaghetti pizza 22, **23**
Stuffed butternut 127
Stuffed peppers 128, **129**
Stuffed sweet potatoes 122
Three-ingredient pasta in a mug **98**, 99
Vegetable lasagne 115
Cheesecakes *see also* Cakes
   Amarula cheesecake 147
   No-bake layered cheesecake 186
Chicken
   Butter chicken pastry parcels 69
   Cheesy rice casserole 102, **103**
   Chicken and barley bake 80
   Chicken and broccoli puff pastry ring 74, **75**
   Jars on the go 100, **101**
   Muffin tin chicken pies 78, **79**
   One-pot chicken and rice 105
   Shredded chicken tacos 81
   Super easy five-ingredient risotto 104
Chocolate
   5-minute mug cake 167

Aero deep-fried ice cream 174
Amarula chocolate crêpe parcels 187
Brownie bowls 164, **165**
Chilli choc spice cream pops 178
Chocolate house 176, **177**
Christmas cake 180, **181**
Christmas cake crumpet stack 183
Coffee-infused vodka soda 210, **211**
Froyo fruit cones 162
Ice-cream sandwich 172, **173**
Layered chocolate rice pudding 150
Molten Aero lava cakes with Bar-One sauce **30**, 31
Peanut butter cookie s'mores pizza 151
Peanut butter stuffed chocolate flapjacks **148**, 149
Peppermint crisp trifle cups **160**, 161
S'mores dip 14, **14**, **15**
Steri Stumpie hot chocolate 184, **185**
Warm whisky volcano 166

Coconut
Amarula coco 208
Cheesy sago poppers 62, **63**
Coconut and lime slushie 202, **203**
Frozen smoothie cake 146

Corn *see also* Maize meal
Chakalaka bread 58, **59**
Cheesy baked fritter stack 111
Cheesy rice casserole 102, **103**
Jars on the go 100, **101**
Mealie meal muffins **38–39**, 39
Rice fritter stack **108**, 109
Sheet pan dinner 88, **89**
Stuffed peppers 128, **129**

Couscous
Stuffed butternut 127

Cranberries
Cran-Brie bites 57
Super yummy breakfast bars 47

Cucumber
Butter chicken pastry parcels 69
Sandwich cake 28, **28**, **29**

Cupcakes *see also* Cakes
Red velvet ice cream cone cupcakes 154

D

Dates
Strawberry smoothie with chia seed pudding 45

Desserts *see also* Sweet treats
Aero deep-fried ice cream 174
Amarula chocolate crêpe parcels 187
Amarula sticky malva puddings **20**, 21
Brownie bowls 164, **165**
Chilli choc spice cream pops 178
Cinnamon and ginger spice cream pops 179
Deep-fried ice cream – SA style 175
Layered chocolate rice pudding 150
Molten Aero lava cakes with Bar-One sauce **30**, 31
Peanut butter cookie s'mores pizza 151
Peppermint crisp trifle cups **160**, 161
Sheet pan pancakes **24**, 25
Warm whisky volcano 166

E

Eggs
Bacon-wrapped breakfast stack 34, **35**
Bovril French toast roll-ups 36
Breakfast baguette 37
Cheesy egg toasty **12–13**, 13
Hash brown breakfast pizza 18, **18**, **19**
White bean shakshuka 41

F

Flapjacks *see also* Fritters, Pancakes, Waffles
Apple flapjacks 158
Peanut butter stuffed chocolate flapjacks **148**, 149

Fritters
Banana fritters with toffee sauce 159
Cheesy baked fritter stack 111
Rice fritter stack **108**, 109

G

Garlic
Chilli con carne skillet 84, **85**
Garlic steak foil pack **82**, 83

Gooseberries
Froyo fruit cones 162
Fruity punch salad mocktail 200

Granadillas
Lemon sorbet soda floats 201
Rooibos and granadilla punch 196
Sparkling granadilla berry smash 217

Grapes
Fruity punch salad mocktail 200

Green beans *see also* Beans
Muffin tin chicken pies 78, **79**
Sheet pan dinner 88, **89**

H

Ham
Bovril French toast roll-ups 36
Calzone dippers 68
Sandwich cake 28, **28**, **29**

Hazelnuts
Froyo fruit cones 162
Fruit and nut yoghurt bars 46

Honey
Honey and cinnamon-infused punch 197
Mint and lime sorbet 192
Rooibos and honey G&Ts **194**, 195
Super yummy breakfast bars 47

I

Ice cream *see also* Sorbet
Aero deep-fried ice cream 174
Chilli choc spice cream pops 178
Christmas ice cream cake 182
Cinnamon and ginger spice cream pops 179
Deep-fried ice cream – SA style 175
Ice-cream sandwich 172, **173**

K

Kiwi fruit
Froyo fruit cones 162
Rainbow popsicles 168, **169**
Strawberry smoothie with chia seed pudding 45

L

Lemons
  Lemon sorbet soda floats 201
Lentils
  Lentil and split pea shepherd's pie 120, **121**
  Spicy lentil and split pea soup 118
  Stuffed sweet potatoes 122
Limes
  Coconut and lime slushie 202, **203**
  Mint and lime sorbet 192
  Strawberry vodka and lime popsicles 198, **199**
  Watermelon and lime slushie 205

M

Maize meal *see also* Corn
  A-maize-zing chakalaka dippers 72
  Chakalaka bread 58, **59**
  Cheesy baked fritter stack 111
  Cheesy maize bites 65
  Maize balls in a creamy bacon sauce 91
  Mealie meal muffins **38–39**, 39
  Pap in a pumpkin 134, **135**
Marshmallows
  Marshmallow and popcorn squares 152, **153**
  S'mores dip 14, **14**, **15**
  Steri Stumpie hot chocolate 184, **185**
Melons
  Fruity punch salad mocktail 200
  Watermelon and lime slushie 205
Mince
  Baked spaghetti pie 94, **95**
  Chilli con carne skillet 84, **85**
  Chilli con carne stuffed sweet potatoes 86
  Mac 'n' cheese boerie bites 56
  Massive mince bun bake 90
  Meatball lasagne soup 76, **76**
  Pasta pie 119
  Veggie nice braai pies 133
Muffins
  Mealie meal muffins **38–39**, 39
  Muffins in mugs 52, **52**
Mushrooms
  Bacon-wrapped breakfast stack 34, **35**

Boerie pies 132
Bread pizza 87
Cabbage rice roll-ups 106, **107**
Cheesy baked fritter stack 111
Cheesy egg toasty **12–13**, 13
Chicken and barley bake 80
Creamy bacon alfredo 97
Garlic steak foil pack **82**, 83
Hash brown breakfast pizza 18, **18**, **19**
Loaded crustless quiche 77
Muffin tin chicken pies 78, **79**
Rice fritter stack **108**, 109
Super easy five-ingredient risotto 104
Veggie nice braai pies 133

O

Onions
  Cheese and onion potbrood 137
  Garlic steak foil pack **82**, 83
  Roast butternut salad 124, **125**
Oranges
  Cran-Brie bites 57
  Festive holiday sangria 212
  Rainbow popsicles 168, **169**

P

Pancakes *see also* Flapjacks, Fritters, Waffles
  Amarula chocolate crêpe parcels 187
  Pancake cake **16–17**, 17
  Sheet pan pancakes **24**, 25
Pasta
  Baked spaghetti pie 94, **95**
  Creamy bacon alfredo 97
  Mac 'n' cheese boerie bites 56
  Mac 'n' cheese burger **92**, 93
  Meatball lasagne soup 76, **76**
  Pasta pie 119
  Sausage and bean spaghetti 96
  Spaghetti pizza 22, **23**
  Three-ingredient pasta in a mug **98**, 99
  Vegetable lasagne 115
Pawpaw
  Banana and strawberry lava smoothies 44
Peaches

Honey and cinnamon-infused punch 197
Whisky peach iced tea 213
Peanut butter
  Frozen smoothie cake 146
  Peanut butter choc power smoothie 42, **43**
  Peanut butter cookie s'mores pizza 151
  Peanut butter stuffed chocolate flapjacks **148**, 149
Pears
  Festive holiday sangria 212
Peas *see also* Split peas
  Chicken and barley bake 80
Pecan nuts
  Christmas cake 180, **181**
  Christmas ice cream cake 182
Peppers
  Rice fritter stack **108**, 109
  Sheet pan dinner 88, **89**
  Sheet pan fajita feast 114
  Stuffed butternut 127
  Stuffed peppers 128, **129**
  Upside-down rice bowl 110
Pies (savoury)
  Baked spaghetti pie 94, **95**
  Boerie pies 132
  Cheesy braai bomb 136
  Chicken and broccoli puff pastry ring 74, **75**
  Lentil and split pea shepherd's pie 120, **121**
  Muffin tin chicken pies 78, **79**
  Pasta pie 119
  Veggie nice braai pies 133
Pies (sweet)
  Farm-style apple pies 156, **157**
Pineapple
  Calzone dippers 68
  Rainbow popsicles 168, **169**
Pizzas
  Bread pizza 87
  Breakfast pizza 40
  Double cheese pizza pinwheel 138, **139**
  Green spinach and split pea pizza 112, **113**
  Hash brown breakfast pizza 18, **18**, **19**

Peanut butter cookie s'mores pizza 151
Spaghetti pizza 22, **23**
Pomegranates
　Festive holiday sangria 212
　Pomegranate sorbet mojito **206**, 207
Popcorn
　Marshmallow and popcorn squares 152, **153**
Pork
　Sheet pan dinner 88, **89**
Potatoes
　Cheesy sago poppers 62, **63**
　Garlic steak foil pack **82**, 83
　Hash brown breakfast pizza 18, **18**, **19**
　Sheet pan dinner 88, **89**
Pumpkin
　Pap in a pumpkin 134, **135**

R

Raisins
　Super yummy breakfast bars 47
Raspberries
　Berry rosé spritzer 216
　Lemon sorbet soda floats 201
　Pancake cake **16–17**, 17
Rice
　Biryani bombs 64
　Cabbage rice roll-ups 106, **107**
　Cheesy rice casserole 102, **103**
　Cheesy rice snacks 73
　Cran-Brie bites 57
　Jars on the go 100, **101**
　Layered chocolate rice pudding 150
　One-pot chicken and rice 105
　Rice fritter stack **108**, 109
　Stuffed peppers 128, **129**
　Super easy five-ingredient risotto 104
　Upside-down rice bowl 110

S

Sago
　Cheesy sago poppers 62, **63**
Salads
　Jars on the go 100, **101**
　Roast butternut salad 124, **125**

Sandwiches
　Croque meneer 26, **27**
　Ice cream sandwich 172, **173**
　Sandwich cake 28, **28**, **29**
Sauces (sweet)
　Amarula coconut caramel sauce 187
　Toffee sauce 159
Sausages
　Boerie pies 132
　Pigs in a blanket 140
　Sausage and bean spaghetti 96
Smoothies
　Frozen smoothie cake 146
　Peanut butter choc power smoothie 42, **43**
　Smoothies four ways 44, 45
Snacks and quick bites
　A-maize-zing chakalaka dippers 72
　Biltong and cheese roll-ups 60
　Biryani bombs 64
　Bread pizza 87
　Butter chicken pastry parcels 69
　Calzone dippers 68
　Caprese pull-apart bread **66**, 67
　Chakalaka bread 58, **59**
　Cheeseburger bites **54**, 55
　Cheesy bread boat 61
　Cheesy maize bites 65
　Cheesy rice snacks 73
　Cheesy sago poppers 62, **63**
　Cran-Brie bites 57
　Cream cheese biltong bites 141
　Double cheese pizza pinwheel 138, **139**
　Easy Caprese pastry squares 50, **51**
　Giant cheese and bov(roll) 53
　Mac 'n' cheese boerie bites 56
　Muffins in mugs 52, **52**
　Pigs in a blanket 140
　Spicy bean dip 70, **71**
Sorbet *see also* Ice cream
　Lemon sorbet soda floats 201
　Mint and lime sorbet 192
　Pomegranate sorbet mojito **206**, 207
Soups
　Butternut soup 126
　Meatball lasagne soup 76, **76**
　Spicy lentil and split pea soup 118

Spinach
　Cabbage rice roll-ups 106, **107**
　Green spinach and split pea pizza 112, **113**
　Jars on the go 100, **101**
　Lentil and split pea shepherd's pie 120, **121**
　Lettuce burgers **116**, 117
　Loaded crustless quiche 77
　Muffins in mugs 52, **52**
　Roast butternut salad 124, **125**
　Sausage and bean spaghetti 96
　Vegetable lasagne 115
Split peas *see also* Peas
　Green spinach and split pea pizza 112, **113**
　Lentil and split pea shepherd's pie 120, **121**
　Spicy lentil and split pea soup 118
Strawberries
　Banana and strawberry lava smoothies 44
　Berry rosé spritzer 216
　Christmas cake crumpet stack 183
　Froyo sarmies 163
　Frozen smoothie cake 146
　Fruit and nut yoghurt bars 46
　Mixed berry sangria 214, **215**
　No-bake layered cheesecake 186
　Rainbow popsicles 168, **169**
　Sheet pan pancakes **24**, 25
　Smoothie swirl popsicles 45
　Strawberry smoothie with chia seed pudding 45
　Strawberry stinger slushie 204
　Strawberry vodka and lime popsicles **198**, **199**
　Whisky peach iced tea 213
Sweet potatoes
　Chilli con carne stuffed sweet potatoes 86
　Lentil and split pea shepherd's pie 120, **121**
　Stuffed sweet potatoes 122
Sweet treats *see also* Desserts
　Chocolate house 176, **177**
　French toast waffles 155
　Froyo fruit cones 162
　Froyo sarmies 163
　Galaxy donuts 144, **145**

Home-made fruit rolls 171
Ice-cream sandwich 172, **173**
Marshmallow and popcorn squares 152, **153**
Peanut butter stuffed chocolate flapjacks **148**, 149
Rainbow popsicles 168, **169**
Red velvet ice cream cone cupcakes 154
S'mores dip 14, **14**, **15**
Steri Stumpie hot chocolate 184, **185**
Three-ingredient home-made fruit juice pastilles 170

T

Tomatoes
Baked spaghetti pie 94, **95**
Cabbage rice roll-ups 106, **107**
Caprese pull-apart bread **66**, 67
Easy Caprese pastry squares 50, **51**
Lentil and split pea shepherd's pie 120, **121**
Loaded crustless quiche 77
Maize balls in a creamy bacon sauce 91
One-pot chicken and rice 105
Pap in a pumpkin 134, **135**

Sausage and bean spaghetti 96
Shredded chicken tacos 81
Spaghetti pizza 22, **23**
Stuffed peppers 128, **129**
Vegetable lasagne 115
White bean shakshuka 41

V

Vegetarian mains
Bean burgers 123
Cabbage rice roll-ups 106, **107**
Green spinach and split pea pizza 112, **113**
Lentil and split pea shepherd's pie 120, **121**
Lettuce burgers **116**, 117
Loaded crustless quiche 77
Rice fritter stack **108**, 109
Sheet pan fajita feast 114
Stuffed butternut 127
Stuffed peppers 128, **129**
Stuffed sweet potatoes 122
Three-ingredient pasta in a mug **98**, 99
Upside-down rice bowl 110
Vegetable lasagne 115
Veggie nice braai pies 133

W

Waffles *see also* Flapjacks, Fritters, Pancakes
French toast waffles 155
Walnuts
Roast butternut salad 124, **125**
Watermelon *see* Melons

Y

Yoghurt
Banana and strawberry lava smoothies 44
Breakfast pizza 40
Butter chicken pastry parcels 69
Froyo fruit cones 162
Froyo sarmies 163
Frozen smoothie cake 146
Fruit and nut yoghurt bars 46
Smoothie swirl popsicles 45

Z

Zucchini
Bean burgers 123
Rice fritter stack **108**, 109
Vegetable lasagne 115

A WORD OF THANKS

A massive thank you to everyone who made this book come to life! In no particular order of contribution or awesomeness ...

Hayley	Francesca	Nwabisa	Karen	Thembi
Chantal	Marylin	Kelly	Baeng	Brenda
Tlholo	Divaksha	Le-Anne	Mbali	Lunga
Julie	Diksha	Dominique	Keegan	Michaela
Cara	Kile	Mokhele	Antony	Rowan
Aviv	Ayanda	Melanie	Laureen	Tall Gary
Loren	Angelique	Leanne	Sasha	Dre
Claire	Cathy	Pralesh	Annie	Liezl
Ant	Dalton	Sayish	Tsepang	Lolly
Caro	Shameema	Olona	Thabang	Holly
Mukundi	Lienke	Mpendulo	Thato	Max
Anneen	Rowena	Mphumu	Julia	
Lisa	Jonita	Waleed	Terri	

From everyone at the Foodies HQ

INDEX | 223

SUNBIRD PUBLISHERS

First published in 2018

Sunbird Publishers
The illustrated imprint of Jonathan Ball Publishers
A division of Media24 (Pty) Ltd
PO Box 33977
Jeppestown
2043

Copyright text © Foodies of SA
Copyright food photography © Myburgh du Plessis
Copyright published edition © Sunbird Publishers

Design & typesetting by Pieter Du Plessis
Cover design by Pieter Du Plessis
Editor Kathleen Sutton
Proofreader Gudrun Kaiser
Food styling by Aletta Lintvelt
Index by Joy Clack
Reproduction by Resolution Colour (Pty) Ltd, Cape Town

Printed by *novus print*, a Novus Holdings company

Foodies of SA asserts the moral right to be identified as the author of this work. All rights reserved. No part of this publication may be reproduced, stored in a retrieval system or transmitted, in any form of by any means, electronic, mechanical, photocopying, recording or otherwise, without the prior written permission of the copyright owner(s).

ISBN 978 1868 4291 03

www.twitter.com/JonathanBallPub
www.facebook.com/JonathanBallPublishers
http://jonathanball.bookslive.co.za/

While every last effort has been made to check that the information in this guide is correct at the time of going to press, the publisher, author and their agents will not be held liable for any damages incurred through any inaccuracies.